HOLY MASS
APPROACHES TO THE MYSTERY

HOLY MASS
APPROACHES TO THE MYSTERY

by

A.-M. Roguet, O.P.

Translated by
CARISBROOKE DOMINICANS

THE LITURGICAL PRESS
ST. JOHN'S ABBEY · COLLEGEVILLE, MINNESOTA
1953

First Edition, July 1953

Nihil Obstat: Hubertus Richards, S.T.L., L.S.S.
     Censor Deputatus

Imprimatur: E. Morrogh Bernard
     Vic. Gen.
     Westmonasterii, die 6a Februarii, 1953

PRINTED IN GREAT BRITAIN
BY ARTHURS PRESS LTD.
WOODCHESTER, STROUD, GLOS.

TABLE OF CONTENTS

PREFACE

Coming after so many recent works dealing entirely with the Mass we hope this little book will not be a repetition of any of them. Actually, this prolific production of books, often of excellent quality, can be divided into three groups. Some explain the ritual, its history and meaning. These run the risk of forgetting the Mass itself in its unity and deep significance at least for some souls who get absorbed in details. Other books less ' liturgical ' or more ' spiritual ' give the preference to commenting on the prayers of the Mass. They sometimes go more deeply into the mystery but they expose themselves to the danger of seeing the Mass as a meditation, rather than an act. Finally there is a whole set of theological productions searching into ' the essence of the sacrifice of the Mass ', analyses that are often very deep, sometimes over subtle in scrutinizing the eucharistic matter and form. They show the central act of consecration by itself under a strong light. They try to discover how a thing that is outwardly a commemorative recital can actually effect a sacrifice and how a transformation that actually touches only bread and wine can bring to pass the sacrifice of Christ who yet remains immortal and unchangeable in his glory. Works of this latter sort propound and set limits to the problem, they too frequently forget to consider the mystery in its breadth.

We here propose to study the Mass, not from its origins and theories but from its ritual acts. We consider that if a Sacrament is a sign then that sign should be legible or audible, so that the essence of the sacrifice could be reached from simple and concrete realities. Again we are of opinion that if our Lord instituted the Holy Eucharist to be the daily food of all Christians and under such common elements as bread and wine, a deep knowledge of the Eucharist should be available to the simplest of believers and not reserved to those who can specialise in dialectic analyses or laboured hypotheses, which things defeat their own ends by their very multiplicity.

The Mass is a simple reality, yet at the same time rich and complex, as are all things that are concrete and alive. In order to get a full understanding of it we must, it seems, go right round the mystery, see it from different angles, complete and correct one idea that one ceremony, or group of ceremonies suggests, by other ceremonies or by the same ones seen from another point of view.

So as not to overlook one of the most essential characteristics of the Mass, we have also tried never to forget that it is an action, a movement, an action that is repeated and that can never be artificially isolated or remain stationary; in short a collective act, the work of a whole people assembled round the priest and the altar.

Again, those who look for a methodical progressive or exhaustive analysis of the Mass here will be disappointed. The Mass is a mystery, that is to say a reality that is infinitely beyond us and that our intellectual reasoning could never reduce to convenient schedule. To get a glimpse of the mystery, to present it under various lights, to bring the Christian soul into contact with it, leaving him the possibility of penetrating further by his own efforts, such has been our ambition. We declare too that we have not treated the Mass merely as an object of contemplation and study, but as a ' mystery of religious worship ' into which one enters by celebrating it or by giving one's attention to it. It can only be known by living it; we know it by assisting at it devoutly, through the reactions it effects in us, much more than by studying it with attention and curiosity at a distance, as something that exists entirely outside ourselves. In this way the present study may contribute to the awakening of a ' liturgical spirit ' in those who read it with sympathy.

The fault of such a method, we admit, is that the book lacks proportion and structure. It is an essay, not a summary.

If these pages have been written out rather rapidly they have been under consideration for a long time and orally expressed under various forms for the last ten years: in two series of conferences at the Priory of St Jacques at Paris; in sermons to the faithful in divers parishes; in many conventual retreats; in numerous diocesan sessions for priests; in a series of talks over Radio-Luxembourg; finally in the assiduous and fervent practice of the running commentary which, inserted during the celebration, is not meant to instruct but rather to direct the prayers of those assembled.

August 25th, 1951.

A.-M. Roguet, O.P.

Chapter I

THE CONGREGATION

Sunday. The church bells are ringing. From all parts of the little country town we see parishioners going towards the same rallying point—the Church.

This is the exterior touch that characterises our Mass at the outset. It has marked it out from the beginning. The very first Christians ' were persevering in the doctrine of the Apostles and in the communication of the breaking of bread and in prayers.' All this is not to be understood as a series of separate exercises but as the essential elements of this ' communication ' where ' the breaking of bread ' describes our Mass. (Acts 3, 42.) Farther on, in the same book, St Luke thus expresses himself ' And on the first day of the week, when we were *assembled* to break bread, Paul . . . . continued his speech until midnight.' (Acts 20,7.) (Here again the same elements. An assembly, the Eucharist, Apostles preaching.)

When St Paul towards the year 55, reproaches the Corinthians for their manner of celebrating the Eucharist which was disorderly and lacking in charity, allusions to this assembling comes repeatedly from his pen: ' You *come together* not for the better but for the worse. For first of all I hear that *when you come together* into one place, it is not now to eat the Lord's Supper.' (1 Cor. 11, 17, 18, 20.) (You are practically denying the Eucharist, Sacrament of unity.) ' Wherefore, my brethren, when *you come together* to eat, wait for one another . . . . that you *come not together* unto judgment.' (1 Cor. 11, 33, 34.)

By 111-113, the younger Pliny sends his report to

Trajan on what he could gather of the life of Christians :
' They are in the habit of *assembling together* on a fixed day
before dawn . . . . '

St Justin, in 150, thus begins his description of Mass.
' On this said day of the Lord, all those who dwell in
towns or fields *assemble together* in *one same place*.' And
before that, he had ended his description of Baptism in
this way: ' After having thus baptised the believer who
comes to us, we lead him to the brethren as we call them
where they are *assembled together* . . . . for the celebration
of Mass.'

Is it an exaggeration to say that for the Christians of
today, this primary idea often passes unnoticed, or at all
events is not appreciated at its true value? We complain
of the parish mob, we seek small chapels; some cling
to their rented sittings, while others stand in a crowd near
the doors, as if to hold aloof from the congregation. Yet
in this coming together there is far more than a mere
practical necessity. There is already a mystery there and
an essential mystery, the very mystery of the Church.
The word ' Church ' means in fact an assemblage and it
was used to denote the gathering together of the faithful
before it was applied to the building where they were.
Again, the word means far more than a building. It is the
sacrament and the parable of the mystery of the Christian
congregation. The stones joined together, ' built ' together, are not only used to give shelter: they outline by
their visible building (Preface of the Dedication) the
unutterable mystery of the ' living stones ' which form
the spiritual temple (1 Peter 2, 5), the ' holy temple in
the Lord ', the ' habitation of God in the Spirit ' ' built
upon the foundation of the apostles and prophets, Jesus
Christ himself being the chief corner stone.' (Eph. 2,
20-22.)

Christ had no other mission, in destroying the sin that had ' scattered the kindreds of the Gentiles ' (Collect of Christ the King) but ' to gather together in one the children of God that were dispersed'. (John 11, 52.) Gathered together, not by chance nor by necessity but to celebrate the liturgy, Christians are the body of Christ; and from that moment Christ, even before the consecration of bread and wine into his body and blood, is there present.

This is the meaning, no doubt, of the salutation that the celebrant addresses so frequently in the course of the Mass to the congregation: *Dominus Vobiscum*. It is usually translated as ' The Lord be with you', and we find its origin in the greeting of Booz to the reapers (Ruth 2, 4). We might remark that the salutation of the risen Christ to his Apostles: *Pax vobis* (John 20: 19, 21, 26) is reserved in the Liturgy to the Bishop because he is first and foremost the representive of Christ in the Church. To priests in a lower rank of the hierarchy, would be reserved a wish of more modest origin (although Booz, ancestor of David and of Christ, master of the harvest at Bethlehem, ' the House of Bread ' is not to be despised as a background for the Eucharistic celebration). And as we translate *Pax vobis* by ' Peace be with you ', so we translate *Dominus Vobiscum* by ' the Lord be with you '.

But *Pax vobis* can just as well be translated ' peace *is* with you ' since these words were uttered by Christ, appearing in the midst of the assembled apostles, and that Christ is ' our peace '. (Eph. 2 & 14.) And besides the *Dominus vobiscum* does not necessarily come from Booz's greeting to his reapers. An angel said to Gideon ' The Lord *is* with thee, O most valiant of men'. (Judges 6, 12.) And above all another angel coming to Mary, said to her *Dominus tecum* which we rightly translate as ' The Lord is with thee '. Why not translate the same salutation simply in the plural by ' The Lord *is* with you '? Did not Jesus himself say ' Where there are two or three gathered together in my name, there am I in the midst of them'? (Matt. 18, 20.)

That is the mystery of the Christian congregation: a presence of Christ that is mysterious but real (although not ' substantial ' as is that which the eucharistic consecration brings into reality) in the midst of those who are gathered together ' in his name ' that is to say in order to pray ' by him, with him, and in him '. Bossuet used to say so well ' The Church is Jesus Christ, but it is Christ spread abroad and imparted'. Where the Church is, there is Jesus. This congregation then deserves great respect, great devotion, and to be greeted as rendering present Christ himself. It is because Jesus is in the midst of them in this way that Christians form a ' chosen generation, a kingly priesthood, a holy nation, a purchased people ' according to St Peter who in another place calls them ' a holy priesthood '. (1 Peter, 2, 5, 9.)

* * *

But we must not think that the Christian Congregation is holy and makes real the presence of Christ from the simple fact of people being gathered together: individual sinners would in that case become divine from the mere fact of their reunion. That would mean crowd mysticism, democratic romanticism after the style of Hugo or de Michelet which Catholic teaching cannot countenance. If these people form a ' holy priesthood ' it is in the first place because they are baptised. Baptism has not only had the effect of washing them individually from the stain of original sin and of giving them grace. It has caused them to be born again as a ' people of God ', as a ' purchased people ', it has made them ' living stones ', it has made them an integral part of the ' house of God '.

If the parochial high Mass, that time of official ' common reunion ', is preceded by the ceremony that is so ignored and neglected, of the sprinkling of holy water during the singing of the *Asperges*, it means that the water of baptism, of which holy water is a reminder, has gathered them into one Church, fit to offer Christ's sacrifice to the Father.

There is another trace, less visible, of this link between Baptism and the Mass and that is the custom, still existing in certain districts, but which has survived everywhere in funeral services, of grouping men and women separately on the two sides of the church. Baptism in ancient times was a real bath (that is the meaning of the word baptism) and it was necessary to be completely unclothed. And so it was administered to men and women separately, each endowed with God-fathers or God-mothers according to their sex whose duty was to undress them, help them down into the baptismal well and up again, to dry them and dress them anew. The newly baptised, carrying candles in their hands made their entry in two rows, men at one side and women at the other, into the basilica where for the first time they were to assist at the entire Mass, and receive Holy Communion. And on Easter night, for the thanksgiving procession to the font they sang the *Vidi Aquam* which we still sing in Paschal time before the High Mass. This aspersion then should remind us every time that if ' the Lord is with us ' it is by reason of our Baptism.

* * *

Fashioned by a new birth, a supernatural birth, the Christian Congregation at Mass is also a hierarchical assembly. It is not a shapeless conglomeration: it is an organised body. This body has a head, a leader. Not only has it an invisible head, Christ, but a visible head: the priest. In a new way, he also makes real the presence of

Christ. That is why to his *Dominus Vobiscum*, the congregation return an equivalent greeting *Et cum spiritu tuo*, ' the Lord is with thy spirit ' which means (the expression is well known to the Jews) ' The Lord is with you also '. The priest is not only incorporated with Christ by baptism so as to form, in union with his brethren, each in his own place and all taken together, the body of Christ; by his ordination he has received personally the power to take the place of Christ, to speak and act in his name to lend him his mouth and hands, to do over again all that Christ did and said at the Last Supper—to the point of being able to affirm in exact truth ' This *is* my body '.

But since Christ is the head of his Church, since he comprises it and sums it up in himself, the priest ordained to take Christ's place by that very fact represents the whole congregation. Not only does he speak to the faithful, he salutes them, exhorts them; but also he speaks in their name to God. He is not their deputy, his power does not derive from them, but he is their representative, ' their ambassador,' as Christ is himself. (cf. Encyclical *Mediator Dei*.) And that is why, right through the Mass (except in devotional prayers more recently added at the Offertory and before the Communion) he never expresses himself in the singular; when he prays he is nothing more than the spokesman of the congregation.

To state precisely the hierarchical order of the assembly, we must also notice the intermediary grades that bind it to the priest: the servers, who do not dispense the congregation from answering and taking part, but who carry out various services in their name (deacon, subdeacon, acolyte): or who are delegated by the celebrant to preach to it the word of God (deacon, subdeacon, lector): or again who keep order in the congregation, regulate its movements, so that it behaves like an orderly and living company (porters). Finally the schola is not primarily a group of professional singers: it is delegated by the congregation, picked men given charge of leading the general singing or of rendering for the congregation the more difficult chants which are meant to feed its thought and help it to join in the praise by its silent and attentive admiration. Again this schola is placed in front of the nave linking it with the altar.

* * *

As Christ is the corner stone of the building, the altar which represents Christ is the most sacred place, the magnetic centre of the congregation; of old this congregation, instead of ranging in rows before it like spectators before a stage or screen, used to encircle the altar. The memento of the living calls the faithful the *circumstantes*: people who are *around* the altar and *standing*: as active, wide-awake, resuscitated participants. One of the features that effectually shows the unity of a congregation and its vitality, and its adherence to the act being carried out at the altar, is the unanimity of its postures and among these postures the frequent standing up all together. To an onlooker who has not become blunted by routine, there is no more shocking sight than Christian congregations that are at variance, where some are kneeling in an attitude of private and penitent prayer whilst others are standing in an attitude of actual and common prayer (or in one of indifference) whilst others finally are sitting down like a passive and weary audience.

Again, nothing is more painful to see than the unrighteous arrangement of those congregations that leave vast unoccupied spaces round the altar whilst all round the holy water stoups and doors are crowds of people who seem to want to hold aloof, not to compromise themselves with the rest, and to remain as alien as possible from all that is going on over there at the altar (it was this state of affairs that inspired the title of Claudel's beautiful study *La Messe là-bas*).

You will say that the worst disturbance of the congregation in Church is due above all to the many late comers. That is true. But to come late to church surely shows lack of respect for the congregation and that one is more anxious to satisfy at all costs one's own obligation than to enter into the spirituality of a congregation at prayer.

In the ancient Church they took care to arrange from the very beginning of the Mass an ordered grouping of the congregation. The ' porters ' made this service an assured one and our liturgical enthusiasts, in default of the clergy, might see to it to-day. Very often too, the congregation was made aware of its unity, thanks to the custom of keeping a ' station ' of which our missals if complete still keep a remembrance. There used not to be as nowadays a great number of Masses, made necessary perhaps—though not always—by the scantiness of our churches, but which break up the congregation. As each church had only one altar so it had only one Mass. If bishops or priests were numerous, they grouped themselves round the principal celebrant and celebrated with him at one altar. On the greatest days there was even a ' station ' (a military term to describe an armed band at attention). All the clergy and people of a city assembled together in one particular church. To make the re-assembling more noticeable they gathered first in another church, the church of the *collection*: of the gathering together or meeting place. There the people were organised by the porters, and processing to the chanting of the Litany of the Saints, a great popular prayer that all could answer, the congregation arrived at the Church of the Station exhibiting to others and to themselves this beautiful sight, so full of meaning, of an organised and united congregation, of a Church on the march in its pilgrimage towards heaven. The Mass could begin and *Dominus Vobiscum* could be said to this baptised crowd. ' The Lord is with you,' my brethren, because you are his body. But also ' The Lord be with you ' could be said because the act that we are going to perform together will make him even more present by uniting you still more, by the mystery of the same oblation of one same sacrifice, of one same repast, to this body of which you already form part.

CHAPTER II

THE SACRIFICE OF PRAISE

Another characteristic of the Christian congregation at Mass is that it sings. The multiplying of ' low ' Masses (a term unknown to the liturgy), the abuse of Masses put to figured music, the repugnance of some pious people to plainchant which seems to them childish and unseemly, ought not to influence us into thinking that singing is an embellishment added on to our liturgy. Chant is essential to it. To celebrate without singing is always an abnormal and mutilated celebration and it should be the exception.

To begin with, singing is a sign of collective prayer. Individual voices join together and blend in the singing. Singing the acclamations intended for the crowd (*Amen*, *Et cum spiritu tuo*, *Deo gratias*) allows it, besides, to join itself to the priest in unanimous adherence. From this point of view dialogue Masses restore one of the original properties of the sung Mass.

But the dialogue Mass remains an incomplete and provisional rendering, it should only be a stage on the way to the return of sung Mass because it lacks another characteristic of singing : this characteristic is the expression of praise. Mass is a feast, it is a ' Sacrifice of praise '.

We get this expression from the Psalms. It comes from Psalm 49 which is an invitation to worship in spirit and in truth, as against the Pharisaism which attaches a sort of magical power to material sacrifice: ' Offer to God the sacrifice of praise: and pay thy vows to the Most High '. And at the end of the same psalm (God is speaking) ' The *sacrifice of praise* shall glorify me, and there is the way by which I shall show him the salvation of God.' It is also found in Psalm 115 designed to accompany a sacrifice of thanksgiving for deliverance from a great trial (mentioned in Psalm 114) ' What shall I render to the Lord for all the things that he hath rendered to me? I will take the chalice of salvation: and I will call upon the name of the Lord. I will pay my vows to the Lord before all his people . . . . Oh Lord . . . . I will sacrifice to thee the *sacrifice of praise* . .'

And this expression describes the Mass, at the heart of the Mass itself, in the *memento of the living*: Thy servants (that we have just named) ' themselves offer thee this *sacrifice of praise* '. This does not prevent the Mass from being at the same time a sacrifice of expiation and propitiation since the text of the Canon goes on: ' They offer thee this sacrifice of praise for themselves and theirs, for the redemption of souls, in the hope of their salvation and they pay their vows to thee,' this last phrase confirming the reference to Psalms 49 & 115.

In actual fact the Council of Trent forbade us to reduce the Mass to a mere sacrifice of praise, ' If anyone should declare the Mass to be solely a sacrifice of praise and thanksgiving . . . and not a propitiatory sacrifice, let him be anathema '. (Denzinger No. 950.) But this does not prevent us from asserting that the Mass is *also* a sacrifice of praise.

At first sight this may astonish us. Is not the Mass a representation of the Cross? Doubtless it is. But the Cross itself is not only a redemptive sacrifice, or rather we must give the redemption its whole positive value. Redemption is not solely the destruction of sin; it is a necessary means for removing the obstacle, but it is not the ultimate aim of the sacrifice.

Man has been created by God solely for his own glory, that is to say, to praise God and to know God with that

admiration that transforms mere knowledge into praise;
and to enable all unconscious creation to sing this praise
' Bless the Lord all ye works of the Lord '. (Dan. 3, 57.)

Sin, to man's shame, prevents him from reflecting back
the divine glory. Sin has wronged the glory of God, not
only because it offends against God's rights; but that it
tarnishes the mirror where the glory of God should be
resplendent with praise.

Redemption removes sin. But for what purpose, except
to reconcile mankind with the Father, to make the
Eternal Father accessible to men? Doubtless it is to
restore God's rights betrayed by sin, but also to enable
man to celebrate the glory of God.

Again the Cross which is an instrument of suffering is
also and above all a trophy of victory. It creates the new
people of God charged and at last able, much more so than
the ancient people of God, to sing his praises proclaiming
his ' wonders '. The ' wonders of God ' is an expression
constantly repeated in the Psalms (cf. 25, 7; 77, 4, 11,
12, 32; 104, 2, 5; 105, 7, 22; 106, 8, 15, 21, 24, 31;
110, 4). St Thomas has put this thought very profoundly
in his treatise on the Sacraments (III, 9, 62, 5) that Christ
by his Passion inaugurated the 'rite of Christian worship'.
The traditional assertion of the Fathers that the Church
(the society dedicated to divine praise) is born of the water
(symbol of baptism) and of the blood (symbol of the Mass)
flowing from the open side of Christ crucified springs from
that. This also explains the surprising epithet of *blessed*
applied to the Passion (*beata Passio*), in the *Unde et memores*,
the prayer in the Canon of the Mass that follows the
Consecration. Sorrowful it is, of course, and yet the
Passion is also a blissful thing, that is to say, gladsome and
glorious, because it brings about God's glory by creating
the choirs of the redeemed who sing the glory of the

Lamb immolated and living. Here I am referring to the Apocalypse, which ends up with songs of praise and which describes heaven under the aspect of a glorious liturgy.

If the Mass represents the Cross, it is by renewing the last supper which involves, contains, and symbolises the Cross in its entirety. Now the Last Supper was a sacrifice offered in the manner of a meal, that is to say a pleasurable action, carried on in a festive atmosphere; Jesus wanted a large room well-furnished: (Luke 22, 12; Mark 14, 15) there is no reason for thinking that the meal was not a good one: Jesus consecrated his body and blood, in a 'Eucharist' which means a prayer of praise and thanksgiving addressed to his Father. We might ask: did not the presence of Judas and the imminence of the Passion cast a gloom over the atmosphere? No doubt, but if we re-read the evangelists with attention, we become convinced that Jesus was in a hurry to send Judas away, to drive away the sinister presence that was poisoning the joy and sweetness of this supreme moment (the exegetes of to-day are agreed in thinking that Judas left the Cenacle before the institution of the Eucharist). Finally at the end of the meal, Matthew and Mark tell us (Matt 16, 30; Mark 14, 26) they sang the Alleluia Psalms, psalms of thanksgiving, from Psalm 112 to Psalm 117 and which therefore include our Psalm 115 (of the *sacrifice of praise*) and the little triumphant 116, *Laudate Dominum omnes gentes* which we sing so often after Benediction of the Blessed Sacrament.

Reproducing the Cross according to the ritual of the Last Supper, our Mass will accordingly have all the characteristics of the Last Supper: it will be all the happier because it is not overshadowed by the proximity of the Passion. Finally we might point out that for the Apostles the Mass recalled the memory not only of the Last Supper which was always the meal above all others, but all the meals that Jesus shared with them, especially those most pleasant ones that followed the Resurrection. In one of his discourses St Peter makes a remark which is at once revealing and very touching. ' Him God raised up the third day: and gave him to be made manifest, not to all the people but to witnesses preordained by God, even to us, who did eat and drink with him after he rose again from the dead '. (Acts 10, 41.)

* * *

We have just explained why the Mass is a sacrifice of praise. It remains for us to see how. The real beginning of the Mass (denoted by the sign of the Cross made by the priest as he goes up to the altar) is the *Introit*, the triumphal song of the procession as it enters. For the most part the Introit is taken from a psalm or at least is sung with a psalm. In the psalms something can be found to fit all the feasts of the liturgical cycle for according to St Denis ' the psalms embrace all that is contained in the Scriptures turned into praise '. And the Prologue of St Augustine's *Commentary on the Psalms* is still more explicit[1]. ' The Psalter is an entire treasury of good doctrine providing on the spot what is necessary in each case. And this instruction is set to melody with delightful song.'

Then to add to the unifying property of ecclesiastical chant : ' Psalmody draws together those who are at loggerheads, it reconciles enemies. How can we still consider one an enemy whose voice has mixed with ours in singing a psalm to God?' . . . Psalms marked the first rudiments for beginners, the growth of those making progress, the confirming of the perfect, *the unique voice of the whole Church*. Psalmody makes solemnity beautiful . . . . psalmody is the angels' occupation, it is the spiritual incense of the heavenly hosts.

[1] This prologue is St. Basil's.

We might say as much of all the psalms that come into the proper of the Mass and are psalms of praise: *Gradual*, *Alleluia*, *Offertory* and *Communion* antiphons: also the fragments of psalms contained in the Ordinary of the Mass: the *Lavabo* taken from Psalm 25: 'I will wash my hands among the innocent: and will compass thy altar, O Lord. That I may hear the voice of thy praise: I have loved, O Lord, the beauty of thy house: and the place where thy glory dwelleth.' After Communion under the species of bread, the priest taking the chalice, says a verse of Psalm 115 'What shall I render to the Lord for all the things that he hath rendered to me? I will take the chalice of salvation and I will call upon the name of the Lord.'

St Paul urges the Colossians to betake themselves to praise in these words: 'let the word of Christ dwell in you abundantly: in all wisdom, teaching and admonishing one another in *psalms, hymns, and spiritual canticles singing in grace in your hearts to God*'. (Col. 3, 16.) What remains of these 'hymns' and 'spiritual canticles' that St Paul numbers with the psalms among the songs of praise? Perhaps vestiges can be discerned with difficulty in St Paul's own writings. But probably our '*Gloria in excelsis Deo*' is one of them. Perhaps that is the 'hymn' that according to Pliny the Christians used to sing to *Christos* as to a God. Before figuring in the Mass, it was sung at the Office, rather like our '*Te Deum*' which is another 'spiritual canticle': these are songs of praise that are not taken from the Holy Scriptures but which have sprung up in lyrical form, in free rhythm, from the heart of the earliest Christians.

The beginning of our Mass contains other elements which we do not usually notice, and which make it a 'sacrifice of praise'. The first is the *Collect* with the other prayers. The body of the prayer consists of a petition that varies.

But this petition is introduced by a cry of praise, a reminder of the divine attributes ' Almighty and eternal God ' . . . ' Almighty and merciful God ' . . . ' O, God who dost manifest thy almighty power above all by thy kindness and mercy ' . . . ' O God, whose providence never fails in its purpose ' . . . ' O God, our refuge and our strength ' . . . But above all, no prayer ever ends without a doxology (a formula of praise) which is full and solemn: ' Through Jesus Christ, thy Son, our Lord, who liveth and reigneth with thee in the unity of the Holy Spirit, God, for ever and ever.' This structure in the prayers yields us two very precious lessons. First of all that petition if we want it granted must begin with praise. And then the doxology teaches us the design or normal ' economy ' of Christian praise. It is addressed to the Father, it is to him *by* this mediator and ambassador of praise, the Son; it expands *in* the vivifying and unifying medium, the Holy Spirit, the soul of the Church. This is the economy of the entire Mass, as we see by studying the Prefaces that open the consecrating and central act of the sacrifice and the great doxology that ends it.

* * *

Now for something that is even more surprising. The first part of the Mass is made a sacrifice of praise just as much by the reading of the Epistle and Gospel. Doubtless these readings are meant for the instruction of the faithful: is not the first part of the Mass the ' Mass of the catechumens ', that is to say of those who are under instruction for baptism? Nevertheless here it is not a question of ordinary instruction. The word of God is not only meant to instruct, or rather if it instructs, it is not merely to enlighten the intellect; it is in order to reveal the greatness of God, and call forth praise. Also the word of God is not only announced, it is proclaimed. The Preface of our Lady's feasts invites us, not only to give thanks but also to *Laudare*, *benedicere*, *et praedicare*, to praise, to bless, to preach. These three words are almost synonymous; for preaching is not merely uttering or stating truths, it is praising and blessing, that is to say, proclaiming and extolling God's wonders. God alone is capable of worthily praising himself and he does it by his Word. If so many Christians lack the spirit of praise, it is because they are not very familiar with the Word of God which they know not how to receive nor how to refer back to God.

Finally the *Credo*, by which we respond to God's word by adhering to it, is not a simple doctrinal pronouncement. Sung by the congregation of baptised souls, it is a profession of faith, it is a confession, that is to say a proclamation of the greatness of God.

We should get the true nature of the Mass out of focus if we only saw in the first part of the Mass a didactic prelude to the sacrifice. That is what some seem to think, to go by the insistence with which they exact perfect understanding of the Epistle and Gospel. Of course if there are readings they are meant to be understood. But in this case it is not so much a matter of rational intelligibility: it is a case of entering into the mystery in the sacrifice of praise, and does not merely require docility of the intellect, as in a catechism lesson but a liturgical attention, an enthusiastic participation.

If the sacrifice of praise is chiefly noticeable in the first part of the Mass (which we prefer, as can now be understood, to call the ' liturgy of the Word ', or the ' Gospel liturgy ') so the entire Mass is a sacrifice of praise. We shall see that the sacrifice properly so-called of the Body of Christ takes place in a ' Eucharist ', in a thank offering. And thanksgiving is a perfecting and completing of praise. But the liturgy of the Word occupies us strongly with the sacrifice of praise. Its very variety teaches us to change and colour our praise according to the seasons or feasts. Whoever systematically comes in at the Offertory, whoever through inattention, for want of a missal, neglects to join in with the liturgy of the Word, is reduced to participating very scantily and monotonously in the eucharistic sacrifice itself. It is true that history, rubrics, casuistry allow us to distinguish two great parts of the Mass. But in reality the whole Mass is a sacrifice of praise for the eucharistic sacrifice properly so-called is already involved and specified by the liturgy of the Word.

*   *   *

This already helps us to understand that the expression ' sacrifice of praise ' that we have used so freely is no metaphor. They may say: What sacrifice, what immolation is there in a sequence of chants and readings? We shall see later that the sacrifice is not necessarily an offering involving bloodshed. The sacrifice is a sacred and sanctifying act; joining in the singing, the work of praising God, listening with fervour to his word, are already dedicating and sanctifying things; they prepare and make perfect the people of God for the sacrifice.

To take the word sacrifice in its everyday meaning: the person who forgets self in the singing, who gives up his own interests to sing the glory of God, who lays himself out to be penetrated to the marrow and transformed by the Word of God, is he not undergoing a purifying and detaching process that might be called a sacrifice, even though it is achieved joyfully? That is perhaps the real reason why Christians lend themselves so seldom to hymns and to praise, they lack, under the guise of dignity and recollection, the unaffected simplicity and forgetfulness of self that is needed for a true sacrifice.

Chapter III

THE EUCHARIST

The Liturgy of the Word is carried on and expands into the Liturgy of the Eucharist. We must now search into the meaning of this word ' Eucharist '.

The ancients for the most part used names that we shall revert to later; the breaking of bread, the Lord's supper, the congregation. Modern folk usually talk of Mass, Communion, and the Blessed Sacrament. But the official term, the one used in the catechism, in enumerating the seven sacraments is the *Eucharist*. This word is of Greek origin, and that gives it a slightly pedantic turn. However it was not invented by theologians. It comes to us straight from the Gospel. It is derived from a verb *eucharistein* which means *to give thanks*. We notice that Jesus gave thanks to his Father at the moment of the miracle of raising Lazarus from the dead (John 11, 41) at the moment of the miracle of the multiplication of the loaves (John 6, 11) which ushered in the Eucharist. Still more did he give thanks to his Father on Maundy Thursday at the moment of giving his disciples the bread that had become his body (Luke 22, 19; 1 Cor. 14, 23) then the chalice of his blood, the eucharistic cup. (Matt. 26, 27; Mark 14, 23.) Before the multiplication of the loaves (Matt. 14, 19; Mark 6, 41; Luke 9, 16) as before the breaking of bread in the presence of the disciples at Emmaus (Luke 24, 30) he ' blessed his Father ' which, under a different word, seems to indicate the same prayer. (In Matt. 26, 26; & Mark 14, 22 it is said that Jesus ' blessed ' in taking the bread at the Last Supper.) But it is the word ' eucharist ' thanksgiving, which has clung to the sacrament of bread and wine, of the body and blood of Jesus given as food and drink.

In thus giving thanks, Jesus merely conforms to a religious custom of the Jews. Whether it was during the Paschal Supper or simply at the meals of family gatherings, the father of the family pronounced a thanksgiving, and a blessing addressed to God, to thank him for his chief benefits : the creation of the world, the gift of food to man, the calling and deliverance of the chosen people, at the time of the first Pasch, which freed them from the Egyptian captivity and the kingdom of idols, to cross the Red Sea and enter the Promised Land.

This was no accidental rite, the Church in her liturgy of the Mass has preserved this act of thanksgiving and given it pride of place. With that the great act of consecration begins, in what we call the Preface. This is not in fact a mere prelude or prologue as the word preface might suggest. It is a solemn proclamation of God's benefits making us enter vividly into the sacrifice. The celebrant calls upon the faithful to lift up their hearts: *Sursum Corda*: Then to give thanks *Gratias agamus Domino Deo nostro*; ' Let us give thanks to the Lord our God '. When the people have answered him. ' It is truly meet, right, and just ' he carries it on and enlarges on it. ' Yes, it is truly meet and just, right and salutary, that we should always and in all places give thanks to thee, O holy Lord, Father Almighty, eternal God '. He then points out the motives for this thanksgiving, which he often draws from the mystery of the feast or season, and he ends by saying that in this way we unite ourselves to the singing of a numberless multitude of angels in heaven, who without ceasing sing ' Holy, holy, holy '. The Mass of which the main phase is opened by the Preface is essentially a thanksgiving.

* * *

But what precisely is thanksgiving? What does the expression ' giving thanks ' mean? We hardly know it outside the Christian vocabulary. That does not mean that it is an obsolete form of speech, which we ought to replace with a more modern one. Some missals with the excuse of adapting themselves, have used the words acclaim, congratulate. They are treacherous. The impossibility of translating the expression only shows us that it expresses a deeply religious feeling with no equivalent in ordinary life.

God is the Creator of all things. All that we have, all that we are, we owe to his Goodness. The first attitude of a devout soul is to acknowledge this debt. Since all has been given to us, in return for everything we have nothing to give. We cannot pay God back. In the same way a child does not pay or reward its parents for having given it life, food, education, and above all their affection. All the same it has no right to be ungrateful. It should acknowledge all it owes them. Its debt can never be discharged. All that they ask is that it recognises the debt and recognises it lovingly. Thanksgiving is just that, it is the opposite of ingratitude. It is not the payment, but the acknowledgement of our total indebtedness to God, an acknowledgement that can only be made by devotedness, by love, and by adoration. Whilst we can clear a debt by expressing our thanks (*remerciement*), thanksgiving (*action de grâces*) has no limit.

This short description gives us an opportunity of suggesting that there are certain elements in thanksgiving. I say merely ' suggest ' and ' certain elements ' for thanksgiving is at the same time so full, so complex, and so simple a thing that one could never adequately define it.

To return thanks then is to acknowledge that we owe everything to God. It is to acknowledge at the same time God's greatness, our sole Creator and Benefactor and our own nothingness; we have nothing and we can give nothing except what we have received in thanksgiving; we admit at the same time that we are incapable of paying our debt and that we are very much aware of this indebtedness. If thanksgiving were due to a fellow-creature, although our superior, it would be somewhat humiliating and painful. But as it refers to God, we joyfully consent to acknowledging not only the gift but our inability to return it. Thanksgiving, far from comprising a humiliation or vexation, is then made up of joy, tenderness, admiration, enthusiasm, as well as gratitude and humility. Far from letting us down, it raises us up; far from saddening us, it fills us with joy.

It is an inexhaustible and unlimited sentiment because it bears upon everything; upon the beauty and richness of the visible world and that is why the sight of beautiful scenery, of a sunrise, of growing plants, of a sleeping child arouses in us an urge for thanksgiving. Again thanksgiving bears upon invisible wonders, the beauty of the human soul, the rich interior life of saints, the fruitfulness of the sacraments and the sweetness of the word of God, the greatness of the Church. Finally, and at its purest, thanksgiving reaches up to God himself, his goodness, greatness, eternal happiness, in one word his glory. In the *Gloria in excelsis* we sing this sublime acclamation; ' We give thee thanks for thy great glory '.

Thanksgiving is of all sentiments the most pure, the most noble, and the most elating because it is the most disinterested that can animate the devout soul. Unfortunately it is not the most natural or the most frequent. How may christians who think themselves good christians spend their time in asking God for benefits, both temporal and spiritual, or in self-pity. We know that Christ has said ' Ask and you shall receive ' and that petition is an integral part of prayer. St Paul, however, knew how to join both together when he said with good psychology ' Be nothing solicitous ; but in everything by prayer and supplication with thanksgiving let your petitions be made known to God '. (Phil. 4, 6.) Surely to associate thanksgiving with petition is a good way of obtaining a hearing since one is showing one's benefactor that one is not ungrateful.

We are accustomed to consider the sacraments as gifts that God gives to our wretchedness, gifts that supply all our needs, and is not man's greatest need a need of thanksgiving? The Eucharist is not only the sacrament that gives us the body and blood of Christ as food; it is also chiefly the sacrament that enables us to offer thanks to God.

Also in the Eucharist our thanks and our gratitude do not just remain sentiments; they take the form of bread and wine. We can offer bread and wine to God because they are the work of our hands; they are the expression of thanksgiving because we could never have manufactured bread and wine had not God first given us earth and heaven, sun and rain, ears of corn and clusters of grapes.

After the consecration we shall say that we are offering to the Father this spotless host ' of thy presents and gifts ', *de tuis donis et datis*. The oriental liturgies have a still stronger way of expressing it; we offer you ' what is yours since it proceeds from you '.

* * *

If we were only able to offer God bread and wine, that is to say a very small fragment of his creation, whilst we are receiving everything from him, our thanksgiving would certainly be ridiculously inadequate. On the contrary we see how the sacrifice of the Mass makes it possible for us to make a return to God that is perfectly worthy of him, because this bread and wine are going to become the very Person of his Son. Now this Son is the great glorifier of the Father, the only one able to offer to God a perfect and substantial thanks-offering. For he is not content with taking our thanksgiving and presenting it to his Father, he *is* himself a thank-offering. True man a creature like ourselves, he knows our nothingness, he shares our wretchedness, he is aware of our powerlessness. God of God, true Son of God, Word of the Father, he has perfect knowledge of the glory of the Father and he is the perfect reflection of this glory. (Heb. 1, 3.) As Man-God, he is the first-born of all humanity, he sums up all creation, he whose whole movement is ' to go to the Father ', he who is the ' Way ' towards the Father, he leads back to the Father all creation and all humanity. And so our Mass is a perfect thank-offering because it offers to the Father not only our singing and our praises, not only the bread and wine, but even the very person of Christ ' in whom we have boldness and access with confidence ' to approach God (Eph. 3, 12), because he ' is the image of the invisible God, the firstborn of every creature. For in him were all things created . . . . All things were created by him and in him . . . . because in him it hath well pleased the Father that all fulness should dwell: and through him to reconcile all things to himself.' (Col. 15, 20.)

This is very clearly expressed in the two prayers that end the Canon. The priest first makes signs of the Cross over the consecrated bread and wine (of old he signed at this moment offerings that were merely blessed; oil, grapes, wax, etc.) saying ' By whom, O Lord, thou dost always create, sanctify, quicken, bless, and give us these good things.' And so all creation is drawn to the Father by the head of creation, Christ. Then the priest making the

signs of the cross with the Host over the chalice, concludes
' By him and with him and in him, is to thee, God, the
Father almighty, in the unity of the Holy Ghost, all honour
and glory for ever and ever.'

* * *

To this great doxology the faithful should reply, *Amen*.
This *Amen* is the apex of their adherence to the thank-
offering and praise that are realised in the Mass in the
Eucharistic sacrifice. St Jerome tells us that in his time,
in Rome, the *Amen* resounded like a thunder-clap. If
now-a-days the *Amen* of the faithful is so timid (supposing
that they say it at all) perhaps it is partly because the meaning
of it escapes them on account of the false translation into a
colourless and resigned ' So be it ' (the fault can be traced
back to the Septuagint Greek translation of the Bible).

Amen does not mean, ' So be it '. When Jesus begins a
statement with *Amen* we do not translate it, ' So be it,' but
' Verily ', i.e. ' In truth '. The *Amen* that ends the sign
of the Cross or the *Credo* is not the answer to a wish. It
is an affirmative conclusion. The old people of Catholic
countries still say ' In the name of the Father and of the
Son and of the Holy Ghost, *Amen*. *Amen* means: It is true.
It carries a hint of enthusiasm. It is the word of faith, of
praise, and of thanksgiving. It is much better not translated
at all. True, it is of Hebrew origin and it is drawn from a
root that means solidarity, confidence. Isaiah says that
God is a God, *Amen*. (Is. 65, 16.) This word has been left
in all languages. It is true we say *Amen* at the end of prayers
which contain a petition; but these prayers finish as we
have seen with a doxology to which the *Amen* is the applause.
The *Amen* that ends sermons, the translation of which by
' So be it ' would drive preachers sometimes desperately
towards ' eternal life '—this *Amen* used to be the conclusion
provided perhaps by the people, to the doxology which

wound up all preaching. For we have seen that ' preaching' was not only explaining or demonstrating, but proclaiming God's praises.

The doxologies with which St Paul sprinkles his epistles all end up with *Amen*.

In the Apocalypse, *Amen* ends the doxologies of the Prologue (Apoc. 1, 6, 7); in the heavenly liturgy the four living creatures answer *Amen* to the praise that ' every creature ' gave to God and to the Lamb (Apoc. 5, 14); in another place *Amen* figures at the beginning of a doxology (Apoc. 7, 12); it cannot mean ' So be it ', it is used in conjunction with the *Alleluia*. (Apoc. 19, 4.) St Augustine preached to his rather surprised listeners that we are going to spend eternity repeating *Amen*, *Alleluia*, because these two words are the only ones capable of expressing our knowledge of divine greatness or the joy that we experience on account of it.

But the Apocalypse contains a rather extraordinary text about the Amen (Apoc. 3, 14). Christ himself is called *the Amen*, the faithful and true witness, who is the beginning of the Creation of God ! He is in person the loving and enthusiastic adhesion that finishes off and sums up the thanksgiving that brings back all creation to the Father. He is the eternal ' Yes ' of creatures giving themselves to the Father to whom they owe everything. St Paul had already said (2 Cor. 1; 19, 20) ' The Son of God, Jesus Christ, who was preached among you by us . . . was not: It is and It is not. But, It is, was in him. For all the promises of God are in him. It is. Therefore also by him, Amen to God unto our glory.'

Chapter IV

THE OFFERING

Our thanksgivings must not remain entirely within ourselves. They are expressed in the first place by offering to God bread and wine.

What does the word offer really mean? It means to set forth or bring before. Such is the primitive meaning of the verb to offer (*ob-ferro*) and of the nouns oblation, offering. In Greek the corresponding term, which for a long time designated the essential part of the Mass, is *anaphore* which means ' lifted upwards '. Both words also comprise an idea of exchange. The offering of bread and wine in the Eucharist has then a very precise and very material meaning. In human language God is always considered to be seated above. God's gifts come down from above. If we want to express our gratitude, to try—impossible though it may be—to pay our debt by a sort of exchange, we shall lift up, present our gifts heavenwards. Remember, before singing the great thanksgiving of the Preface, the priest addresses the faithful: *Sursum corda*, lift up your hearts ! It is certain that God, pure spirit, is at the same time both everywhere and nowhere, but nothing need prevent men from representing God as dwelling in the heights. We sing in the *Gloria* and in the *Sanctus*, ' Glory be to God in the highest '.

We shall not be surprised then, to see the priest at the beginning of the eucharistic sacrifice, properly so-called, raising towards heaven the host placed on the paten and the chalice filled with wine.

It would be a great mistake, however, to think that this gesture once accomplished, the offering is over. In reality the whole Mass is an offering, that is to say, a raising up of our gifts. When the Bishop ordains a new priest and enumerates his chief duties, he says quite simply *Sacerdotem oportet offerre*—The priest should offer—and this one sober word describes the celebration of Mass. When the consecration is over the priest says a magnificent prayer of which the principal word is *offerimus*: we offer. It is not sufficient to render present on the altar by the consecration the body and blood of Jesus, the victim, they must be offered up to his Father.

We must beware of a mistake at this point. I have said the offering consists externally in a lifting up of gifts. But what is known as the ' elevation ' is no offering. This elevation, which immediately follows the consecration and at which the bells of the altar boys and the stillness and silence of those present give striking effect, this elevation was inaugurated in the 13th century by the bishops who were building Notre Dame de Paris, simply with the intention of showing the Host to the faithful. In ancient times it did not exist and had no reason to exist, since Mass was celebrated facing the people. It has never existed in the East. But there is another elevation in the Mass, the one called, most unfortunately, ' the little elevation '. In reality it is the more important of the two. This is not with the object of showing the Host to the people but to offer it to the Father. It is the end and climax of the canon of the Mass, which from one end to the other has been nothing but an offering by men, of the sacrifice of Christ to the glory of his Father. The ' little elevation ' concludes this offering in a particularly significant and solemn way and all the faithful join in—or alas ! ought to join in—by a resounding *Amen*.

And so the Mass from beginning to end, is essentially an offering.[1] In this case of what use is the offertory?

It is only actually a preparation for the offering, a bringing together of the gifts of bread and wine. Doubtless we offer these because they are ours, we give them as gifts to be sacrificed. This is only a beginning, an indispensable condition. The bread and wine are not going to remain as such. God will take them, he will make of them body and blood of his Son. Jesus, because of and under the appearances of bread and wine, will offer himself to his Father for the salvation of the world. Jesus offered himself and sacrificed himself both at the Last Supper and on the Cross. It is that offering that the Mass renews. The real offering then takes place at the consecration and not at the offertory.

This is not all. The Mass does not end at the consecration. It continues in prayers and actions that are too seldom explained. It is not enough that Christ offers himself invisibly. Visibly it is the Church, in the person of priest and people, who offers the sacrifice. All the prayers that follow the Consecration are meant to allow the Church to offer the sacrifice of Christ and to offer with him. In fact Christ is never alone. Since Calvary and Pentecost he has made of all men, especially the baptised, that is to say the whole Church, a Body, of which he is the head. The body cannot live without the head. The head cannot help dragging the body with it wherever it goes. At Mass then, it is not only Christ who offers himself and is offered; the Church, that is all of us, offers, offers itself and is offered with him.

Doubtless this will help us to correct our way of thinking and behaving with regard to the Eucharist and the Mass. In

[1] It is also more than that, but one cannot say everything at once and it does not prevent the Mass from being entirely an offering and a sacrifice.

the Mass alone we see a sacrifice accomplished by Christ, which we need only watch while praying to benefit by its fruits. In that case, it matters little if at Mass we are thinking of other things, or saying our rosary. Christ is doing everything. If that is all Mass is, why need we be present at all? Would it not be sufficient for some priests here and there to celebrate it? Whether we are present or whether we stay at home the sacrifice of Christ will be offered none the less. But if Mass consists in the whole Church offering up Christ and offering itself with Christ then we can see that all baptised souls should be present at Mass—or rather not that they should merely be present as passive spectators, but that they should join in and take an active part in it.

Perhaps in the Eucharist we see too exclusively holy communion, the coming down to us of a wonderful gift of God that we have nothing to do but receive, contenting ourselves with merely opening our mouths. If the Eucharist is first of all a thanksgiving, an offering, it is not only a coming down of God to man, it is also a raising of man to God. It is not enough to be a recipient, we must also give ourselves, we must offer ourselves up.

Now this is the fundamental attitude of the devout soul. God wants us to offer ourselves, to give ourselves to him. He is not contented with our respect, our obedience, nor even with our prayer, if in respecting, obeying, or praying to him, we remain our own masters shut up, in a sense, within ourselves. The Mass does not merely require that we should offer bread and wine, as material inanimate objects; it does not ask us to offer Christ, as an adorable person, of course, but outside of us. It invites us to surrender ourselves, and this is for a very simple reason; it is a sacrament of charity, of love. There is no love if one is content to give external goods however precious. Alms have been described as refinement of contempt and that is true if one has been content to give money while withholding one's own heart. Love does not consist of giving but of self-giving. When he died upon the Cross, Jesus gave nothing outside himself, but he did give himself entirely. Had he not warned us ' Greater love than this no man hath, that a man lay down his life for his friends.'

NOTE ON THE PROBLEM OF THE OFFERTORY

These last years we have seen a movement developing that tends to exaggerate the value of the offertory. Sermons and Mass commentaries have insisted on the human significance of the gifts, on the symbolism of the drop of water, etc. ' Offertory processions ' have been organised where the most whimsical offerings are paraded—even parents ' offered ' by their own children.

This tendency has an explanation. The offertory especially when, as in ancient Rome, the faithful brought their gifts to the altar, makes it easy for those assisting at Mass to show their participation. Bringing various gifts seems to show, more than the simple elevation of a host provided by the sacristan, the inserting of the Mass into the whole human life—the duty of coming to Mass not only with sentiments of becoming piety, but with a generous and real effort to christianise every day life. We might well say that it is easier to exploit the human side of the eucharistic mystery than to explain what is more central in it and more divine.

Unfortunately this tendency borders on a singular deformity of the meaning of the Mass, so as to make of it an offering of man rather than an offering of Christ. We have assisted at Masses with a running commentary, etc., where the offertory was emphasized by an endless text, whilst the *Unde et memores*, the *Supplices* or the little elevation were hardly noticed, if not entirely passed over.

Really the offertory is nothing more than the bringing of gifts, a material preparation for the sacrifice accompanied by prayers. These prayers, comparatively recent ones, are merely a rather servile addition to the Canon. All the same, there is a point there that should not be missed; if we ask God to look favourably upon these gifts, it is because Christ is already seen in them. On this score we often speak of anticipation, or more learnedly of *prolepsis*. This seems to be superfluous. There would not be any anticipation if the liturgy after the manner of theology, influenced by the casuistry of ' defects ' in the Mass, would distinguish carefully between consecrated and unconsecrated gifts. But it does not do so. The Liturgy hardly knows the ' before ' and the ' after '. Genuflexions after the consecration are of later date. The *Secrets* speak in a general way of gifts which are not yet consecrated, not only as if they were consecrated already, but as if the faithful had already received them. In the Byzantine liturgy, the offerings that are brought in at the ' Great Entry ' (corresponding to our offertory) are venerated by the faithful just as we venerate the Blessed Sacrament. And Rome has forbidden anyone to worry the Uniates on this point. If more notice had been taken of this indifference in the liturgy with regard to the ' before ' and ' after ' there would not have arisen false problems or useless stiffening of real problems concerning the Oriental ' Epiclesis '. (An invocation of the Holy Ghost to ask him to sanctify the gifts after pronouncing the words of the Institution.)

In the Mass, if we are seeing it from the point of view of efficaciousness, everything happens at the one consecration. This not only brings about the true presence in effecting transubstantiation, it renders present the immolated Christ, it immolates him sacramentally. Or, if you will, Christ immolates himself, he offers himself (as long as one admits, as seems certain to us, that the offering and the immolation are not two really separate acts.) At the same time, with himself he offers his body, the Church. We might even say that the essential quality of Communion becomes a fact at the consecration; by it we all, however great our numbers, form one sole body of Christ.

The mystery however must be expressed and developed sacramentally to be accessible to man. What happened in a moment of time will be spread out over all time. The unique sacrifice will comprise phases (rather than parts or ' acts ' as in a drama) which will show up its inexhaustible riches. The *Unde et memores* will enumerate the various mysteries brought into being on the altar by the one sole ' mystery of faith '. Communion will bring together or complete in a most real fashion, the union of all and each to the body and in the body of Christ. The offering of Christ and of the Church with him will be expressed in the *Unde et memores* (of which the principal verb is ' *offerimus* ') and in the *Supplices*. That is the actual offering and it does not come from our more or less devout sentiments, from our gifts however varied and abundant, but from the very objective fact in a way outside ourselves and prior to our participation in the Mass that being baptised we have become members of Christ making one with him.

The preparing of the gifts, called the offertory, may be considered as a ritual expression of this offering which only becomes a fact at the consecration; whilst the communion which follows brings into play one of its most important effects (for in any ritual taking place in time there must be a ' before ' and an ' after ' although there is no such thing in the mystery itself).

All that is normally said of the offertory can therefore

be approved as long as we see in it a ritual expounding of the only offering that matters; that of Christ and the Church at the consecration.

But error can creep in, if we give this offertory first place as a sacrificial act, self-sufficing; and if we see in it the offering of man apart from the offering of Christ. To hear some commentators on the Mass, one might think that after the offertory everything that was essential had been done and that the faithful could, strictly speaking, disperse before the consecration which no longer concerns themselves, but Christ alone.

As to the offering of various gifts we must make a triple distinction. If it concerns bread and wine that will be used in the sacrifice, nothing is more praiseworthy. If it means divers commodities of the sort to be consumed either for worship (bread, wine, wax, oil) or for charitable works (commodities such as clothes or firewood for the poor), they can bring those to the offertory and this gesture is traditional. In that case it must be clear that they are not bringing an oblation, but coming to seek a blessing, a ' eulogy ' as in the venerable custom of ' pain bénit '. Finally offerings of implements, cradles, etc., are quite unjustifiable. In the liturgy nothing is ' offered ' to be restored afterwards to the owners. There are many blessings provided in the ritual for these things, but outside of the Mass. It would be better to keep out of the Mass also the offerings of the second category if, because of their quantity, they give an exaggerated importance to the offertory as regards the rest of the Mass.

Chapter V

THE EXCHANGE

The Eucharist is the sacrament of giving. It is doubly so. It is the sacrament of God's gift to men. It is the sacrament of man's gift to God.

God gives himself to men. In this little phrase there is all the difference between an abstract idea of God and the revelation that God has made to us of himself in the Scriptures. A philosopher can arrive by reasoning at the conception of a Supreme Being, a master Creator of the universe and even of a Providence. The Jews, who had had the personal revelation of the one true God, knew that God was full of solicitude for them, even of tender love. For the God of the Old Testament was not solely, as is too often asserted, a God of fear; many passages in the Prophets already show him as a fatherly and very loving God.[1]

But it was reserved to Jesus Christ to announce to us his Gospel, that is joyful news, the incredible news of the gift of God to men. This gift is himself. As St John says in one of the most bewildering of the Gospel sayings: ' God so loved the world, as to give his only begotten Son '. (John 3, 16.) Such is the foundation, if one might say so, of the mystery of the Incarnation, of God becoming man; such great radiance, such overflowing goodness towards humanity on the part of God that he gives himself to it, that he unites himself to it in the most intimate way imaginable. He espouses this humanity in such a manner as to be

[1] cf. for example Isaiah, 40-45; 54-66: Jeremiah 31, 33; Ezech: 34; Osee 2, 11, etc.

one with it, in the unity of one sole person, our Lord Jesus Christ, true God, true man.

Jesus Christ is truly a gift of God to men. Being God, he has been given to us gratuitously, without any rights or merit on our part. Again, he has not been shown or lent to us; he has been given to us, he belongs to us, he is ours, having our human nature, our flesh with all its weaknesses except sin, having known poverty, fatigue, hunger and thirst, betrayal and death. He shared men's meals and like other men was laid in the tomb.

When Jesus returned to heaven we were not left orphans, he gave us his Spirit, the Holy Ghost, one of whose names is rightly the ' Gift '. It is the Holy Spirit who makes God dwell in us because he is love. This presence and this life of God abiding within us by the Holy Ghost is also called grace. It was grace that Jesus was speaking of when he said to the Samaritan woman: ' If thou didst know the gift of God '. To this woman who was eagerly seeking love and only finding it in sin which is the caricature and poison of love, Jesus offers a love that quenches thirst instead of increasing it; ' If thou didst know the gift of God and who he is that saith to thee: Give me to drink, thou perhaps wouldst have asked of him, and he would have given thee the living water . . . He that shall drink of the water that I will give shall not thirst for ever. But the water that I will give him shall become in him a fountain of water, springing up into life everlasting.' (John 4, 8-15.)

We come now to the Eucharist. It sums up and contains all the gifts of God to men. Jesus Christ is really present therein and is given to us so entirely as to become our food. In the very words in which he declared his presence, Jesus at the same time declared that he was giving himself. ' This is my body which is given to you, Take and eat ye all of this.' The Eucharist gives us Jesus Christ offered up, that is to say given entirely: There is no greater love than to give one's life for one's friend. It does not only give us his sacrifice but Jesus whole and entire with his body and his soul, his blood, his humanity and his divinity, and all his mysteries.

Finally, in holy communion, Jesus is not only given us so that we eat his flesh for Jesus says with respect to that ' The flesh profiteth nothing ' (John 6, 64), but so that we should be filled with his spirit and his grace. In a beautiful antiphon for the feast of Corpus Christi, we sing the words of St Thomas Aquinas: ' *O Sacrum Convivium.* O Sacred Banquet in which Christ is received . . . the soul is filled with grace and a pledge of future glory is given to us '. See how the Eucharist is above all things the gift of God to men. All the sacraments are certainly gifts of God but this one surpasses and sums them all up because it contains the greatest gift, Jesus Christ.

* * *

If the Eucharist is the gift of God to men, it should be the gift of men to God. Have you noticed that in Jesus's dialogue with the Samaritan woman, before saying to her: ' If thou didst know the gift of God ' Jesus begins by asking the Samaritan woman: ' Give me to drink '.

God gives to us, God gives himself to us. But he also wishes us to give to him, to give ourselves to him. His gift is not invisible; it is his Son made Man, visible in our midst. Our own gift cannot be merely a spiritual gift. It must be visible, it must be a sign, that is to say a sacrament. This sacrament is the Eucharist. We give God our presence at Mass, our singing, our prayer, our attitudes, bread and wine. Of course, as we have already said all that has been given us by God. So the prayer after the consecration says,

' We offer unto thy most excellent majesty of thy presents
and gifts a pure host.'

In olden times in Rome this gift of the faithful was
carried out in a particularly significant manner. They came
in procession to the altar carrying bread and wine, also oil,
wax, fresh fruits. One part of these gifts was directly used
for the sacrifice, being consecrated. Another part was used
for the poor. The last part finally was for the maintenance
of the clergy. The liturgy has kept these gifts in mind. In
passages of the Mass the bread and wine, even after the
consecration, are often called *dona*, *munera* gifts and presents,
because the fact that they have been brought by the
faithful is not forgotten.

We might regret the old custom of a procession by which
the faithful brought their gifts to the altar. But do not
forget that this ceremony is maintained in a simplified
and evidently less poetic form, quite simply by the collection. We might be right no doubt in protesting against
endless, multiplied indiscreet collections. But we should
be wrong to want to exclude the collection from the
Mass. It is an integral part of it. Let us not see in it a
sordid necessity but rather a devotional gesture, and again,
a sign. What counts is not the amount we give, but the
depth of generosity. Remember how Jesus watched a poor
widow putting a very small piece of money into the
temple treasury. ' Verily I say to you, that this poor
widow hath cast in more than they all. For all of these
have of their abundance cast into the offerings of God; but
she of her want hath cast in all the living she had.' With a
penny or whatever corresponds to it nowadays—or with
a big check, we must give from our hearts so as to have
a share in the sacrifice of him who has given himself.

Paul Claudel in the ' offertory ' of his beautiful poem
' *La Messe la-bas* ' makes the celebrant say: Now the plate

is held out, have you nothing but that miserable penny, that nameless coin under the dirt and the only purse that opens?

Why defraud our God of what is his own, his property ?

* * *

If we offer God bread and wine, and afterwards the body and blood of Christ present under their appearances, we expect God in return to fill us with all kinds of blessings. In this way the Mass is a deed of exchange. The liturgy often uses this word in the prayer of the Mass, the secret, where we ask to receive benefits in return for what we are offering. ' O God, who by the sacred intercourse (*exchanges*) of this sacrifice makest us partakers of the one supreme Godhead, grant we beseech thee, that as we know thy truth so we may follow it in worthiness of life ' (IV Sunday after Easter and XVIII after Pentecost.)

In the ancient liturgy of Rome, these exchanges of the Mass were very striking. The faithful came to the altar in procession twice. The first time, at the offertory, they came to present their gifts. After the sacrifice, they came in the same order to take back their gifts, but these had been changed. The faithful who had merely offered bread and wine, received in exchange the body and blood of Christ. In place of human offerings that they had brought, they were given the bread of eternal life and the chalice of salvation. It was a true exchange but what a profitable one! We can never lose when exchanging with God; to anyone who gives generously he returns a hundred-fold and more!

That idea of exchange appears already in the fundamental mystery of Christianity; the incarnation. God and men are no longer separated by an insurmountable abyss. Between them a bridge has been thrown, a commerce—in the noblest sense of the word—has been established. This is what the Church sings in one of the most beautiful antiphons of the Christmas season. ' *O Admirable Commercium*. . . O admirable interchange! The Creator of mankind assuming a living body, deigned to be born of a virgin; and, becoming man without man's aid, bestowed on us his divinity ' (antiphon for 1st vespers of the Circumcision). We find the same idea again in one of the Christmas prayers which has been placed in the ordinary of the Mass for the blessing of the water that the priest mixes with the wine in the chalice: ' Grant, O Lord, that we may share in the divinity of him who has partaken of our humanity.' The Mass only continues and perfects this exchange; our bread and our wine, gifts of man, become the flesh and blood of God, and they are given back to us to become our flesh and blood, and so to make us divine.

These considerations may appear somewhat subtle. We might notice however that without interchange there is no life, even physiologically. Without interchange there is no social life, nor even cultural or intellectual life.

Of what does the nourishment and growth of a plant consist if not in the exchange with the earth where it has taken root and which it will come back and nourish when it decays? In what does breathing consist if not in an exchange? Any being shut up in itself, drawing nothing from the surroundings in which it lives and giving nothing in return, could neither grow nor develop. Flint knows no change but all living things live by exchanges.

What else is instruction, mental culture, literary or artistic life, reading, conversation, but an exchange of ideas? What else is trade, social life but an exchange of service? Society is unhealthy when ruled by injustice, it is always the same people who give and the same ones who receive without any true exchange between Capital and

Labour, manual workers and intellectuals, the simple and the learned. A family is only alive and happy when such intercourse rules there. Of course children receive everything from their parents but they should make them any return in their power, first of all of affection and respect, and later of support and assistance.

In the same way there is no spiritual life if there is no interchange. A soul shut up in itself that looks for nothing from some higher being is a dead soul. A soul that only prays to God to receive his favours, but who never thanks him, offers him neither praise nor thanksgiving, is a soul living a very languid and mediocre life. Here we touch upon the absolute necessity of prayer. Prayer is not a humiliating and interested beggary. True prayer is nothing more than continual intercourse with God. Prayer has been very well defined as the breathing of the soul. Just as the body breathes by interchange, by a double movement of breathing in and breathing out, so the soul breathes when it inhales God by petition and when it gives back to God some of its own gifts by thanksgiving and praise.

Our Lord taught us the power of prayer in a parable that must be read entirely in order to be understood fully. It is found in the gospel for the Rogation days. (Luke 11, 5-13.) Christ gives us as example a friend who knocks on his friend's door in the middle of the night asking for bread. The sleeper ends by getting up so as to have peace. Then Jesus suggests the picture of a child asking its father for something to eat and certainly not receiving a stone instead of bread, a scorpion instead of a fish. If we stopped there we might think that prayer only asked of God temporal things or personal advantages. But read the gospel to the end: ' If you then, being evil, know how to give good gifts to your children how much more will your Father from heaven give you the good Spirit to them that

ask him '. You understand: the Holy Spirit. True prayer
consists not in asking God for this or that happiness, success,
health, even eternal salvation but the Holy Spirit, The
Spirit, that is to say, breath, inspiration. As the psalm has
it: ' I opened my mouth and panted because I longed
for thy commandments. ' (Psalm 118, 131.) Prayer confers
upon us this mysterious breathing, this holy and good
Spirit which allows us to breathe in God and breathe out
God, to be in a state of interchange with him.

* * *

We see here how the Mass is a school of perfect prayer.
It is not one uniform movement, it is a perpetual coming
and going. Before the Mass begins we ask pardon with the
Confiteor. Then we praise God in the *Introit*. Again we
declare our wretchedness in the *Kyrie Eleison*. Then we
glorify God by the *Gloria*. We ask his help in the *Collect*.
In the Epistle we listen to the teaching of the word of God.
We pause and meditate on it in the *Gradual* and *Alleluia*.
We are taught by the *Gospel*. Our consent to it and reaction
is shown in the *Credo*. In the *Offertory* we bring our gifts
to the altar. And all that follows is a close fabric of thanksgiving and petition for all the needs of the church. Christ
once given to us in the Consecration, we offer him to
the Father for his glory. Finally we receive him as food.
The Mass finishes with one last thankoffering. And so the
Mass is a perpetual exchange, an incessant coming and
going, a ladder that is more sublime and more mysterious
than Jacob's which was standing on the earth and the top
thereof reaching to heaven; the angels also of God
ascending and descending by it; and the Lord leaning
upon it. (Gen. 28, 12.)

Provisionally I have left aside that interchange, also
indispensable, that should reign between Christians by

brotherly love. So far we are confining ourselves to the fact that the Mass teaches us to break down the crust of egoism which too often numbs the soul, so as to make us exercise a vital intercourse with that God who is not only a master to be adored and entreated, but a Father who gives us life and expects to be given our love in exchange.

CHAPTER VI

BROTHERLY LOVE

We saw in the first chapter that the Mass appears in the first place as an act of the community, of the Church.

Unfortunately, the word ' Church ' still too often suggests to our minds a material building or an administrative structure. Or perhaps we imagine the Church to be nothing else than the clergy with its complex hierarchy, its different religious orders, etc. The true idea of the Church is very much simpler, very much wider and much more beautiful. The Church is the gathering of all believers, so closely united that they form, not merely one sole society, or one sole family, but one spiritual organism and according to a striking expression that we owe to St Paul: one body of which the head, the leader, is Christ whose soul is the Holy Spirit.

Two sacraments make up this body: First Baptism aggregates us together, now some, now others, in proportion to our generations. But for each one of us this incorporation is realised once for all, or rather is inaugurated at Baptism. What daily renews this unity and draws it together is the Eucharist. It is the sacrament of unity, the sacrifice of the Church, that is to say of the gathering together of all christians. The secret for Corpus Christi puts it clearly and briefly ' Unto thy Church, we beseech thee, O Lord, grant the blessings of unity and peace mystically set forth by these gifts we offer '. The consecrated bread shows forth and contains the physical body of Christ but it shows forth and contains still more mysteriously what we call his mystical body, that is to say, the unity of all christians in Christ.

Besides, originally this expression ' mystical body ' meant precisely the eucharistic body. If ' mystical body ' has ended by meaning the union of Christians it is because that union is principally shown forth and produced by the Eucharist.[1]

Between the Mass and the Church there is not some accidental connection but an essential relationship. It is the Mass that brings the Church together, it is the Mass that makes the Church just as it is the Church that offers the Mass and that offers itself at the Mass.

This brings us back to the fact that this is the sacrament and the mystery of brotherly love. For the Church is not just any society whose unity consists in a code of external laws. It is a love company. Its leader, who is its means of unity, Christ, does not hold his power merely as an authorised commander, but also by his pre-eminence of love. It is because he has loved men to the utmost, because he has given the greatest proof of love, to die for them, that Christ draws them together. The great commandment that he left to his disciples and which he left them at precisely the very moment of instituting the eucharist, of celebrating the first Mass, was to love one another as he had loved them.

This explains many features in the celebration of Mass. It is not a solitary action, it is a gathering. If the faithful are asked to group themselves together near the altar, to answer the priest, to adopt postures in common, it is not just to give more of life and beauty to the functions; it is chiefly because the sacrament of unity should be intimated in the unison of bodies, voices, attitudes, and more deeply still by the union of hearts.

[1] cf. H. de Lubac, *Corpus mysticum*.

Why did they, in olden times, at the offertory send out
the catechumens, Jews, pagans, public sinners? It was
just because the sacrament of unity should be celebrated
solely by those who had been gathered together into one
company by baptism or who had not been separated by
grave faults. Why is it, when the Canon of the Mass is
finished and the Communion draws near that the ' Pater '
is solemnly said? It is because that prayer puts on our lips
not ' my Father ' but ' our Father ' implying that we are
all brethren. It is also because in that prayer we say
' Forgive us our trespasses as we forgive them that trespass
against us '. We should not go to the eucharistic communion with thoughts of rancour, jealousy or contempt.
According to the greatest theologians, what makes
communion a sacrilege is not so much the fact of receiving
Christ, who is most holy, into a soul defiled with sin.
Christ in glory is above contamination; and how could a
soul that is soiled defile this body which is impassable and
glorious after the resurrection? What constitutes the
sacrilege is the horrible lie of approaching the sacrament
of unity while keeping up an attachment to sin which is
nothing more than division and a default of love and union
with God and our brethren.

All the preparations for communion after the ' Pater '
are meant to remind us of the essential duty of brotherly
love. The ritual of breaking of bread, formerly so long
and important, to-day reduced almost to nothing by the
use of unleavened bread and hosts that are cut out in
advance, has a deep sense of unity. Allegorical interpretations which throughout the centuries have falsified
explanations of the liturgy have tried to see in it a symbol
of the passion. Now St John took care to point out to us
that for Jesus, as for the paschal lamb, ' You shall not break
a bone of him ' (John 19, 36; Exod. 12, 46; Num. 9 12.)

And theologians firmly maintain that when the host is raised up, locked up, divided, it is not Christ himself who is raised up, locked up, divided, but the sacred species. The ceremony in question is never called the ' breaking of Christ ' but ' the breaking of bread '. Why then should we not interpret it as having reference to the simple and grand gesture of the father of the family at table dividing up the same loaf among all his children?

Some of these fragments were used as *fermentum* (the leaven of concord and of charity): acolytes like St Tarcisius used to carry them hung in linen bags, round their necks, to priests or bishops, often near at hand, sometimes at a distance, who would join this bread received from their brethren to that of their own sacrifice. Two bishops would show in that way that they were ' in communion ' with each other. The expression has a very definite meaning.

Again before Communion the *kiss of peace* was given, begun at the altar and passed on among all the faithful. It was applying our Lord's own precept, formerly carried out at the offertory so as to obey the gospel word more strictly; ' If therefore thou offer thy gifts at the altar and there thou remember that thy brother hath anything against thee leave there thy gift at the altar and go first to be reconciled to thy brother; and then coming thou shalt offer thy gift '. (Matt. 5, 23, 24.)

Everyone used to come to the altar, at that time there was only one, in procession—sign of unity—and singing—another sign of unity and charity. How is it that nowadays we still tolerate at Communion a helter-skelter of the faithful hurrying to get there first and treading on each other's feet? The organising of a nice procession, grave, orderly and engaged in singing is not only a matter of good order, it would bring home to the faithful the fact that

eucharistic communion is a ritual that expresses and brings
about fraternal charity and church unity.

We communicate at the one altar. The 'holy table'
is the altar even though the laity out of respect for the
altar where only priests have access, have to stop at a
barrier that scandalises some people but which is traditional. Attached to this railing there should be a 'communion cloth' a duplicate of the altar cloth (the cloths
that cover the altar says the *Pontificale*, in the ordination
of a subdeacon, are symbolic of the christian people united
to Christ who is symbolised by the altar). The recent use
of a 'communion plate' is justified by respect for the
sacred particles. It does not do away with the cloth.
Besides, the use of a plate alone has the objection of
suggesting a series of private repasts whereas communion
is a banquet. Let the acolyte hold the plate and the communicants hold on to the communion cloth, useless but
highly significant as a sign of partaking in a meal among
brethren. There is finally a little ceremony of deep import:
at a pontifical Mass, the Bishop before placing the host
on the lips of the communicant presents his ring to be
kissed. That ring is a covenant, the sign of the bishop's
espousals with the Church (as Christ's representative).
The communicant in kissing this sign of union and unity
declares that his communion with the body of Christ is
also a communion with the Church.

* * *

On Maundy Thursday and Corpus Christi the Epistle of
the Mass gives the passage where St Paul recalls the
circumstances of the institution of the Eucharist by Christ
at the Last Supper. Now St Paul does not give us this
doctrine just to draw out a theoretical teaching. It is there
as a reaction against the abuses that were prevailing in the

Church at Corinth. They practised there a rite that has disappeared to-day called the ' Agape '. This Greek word ' *Agape* ' means brotherly love, charity. It describes a family meal that the faithful took all together and which ended in the celebration of the Eucharist. That Agape had degenerated. They were eating at small tables instead of the rich and the poor sharing together. Some stuffed whilst others went hungry. So, says St Paul, you cannot call it celebrating the Lord's Supper, since you are so gravely wanting in charity.

We read this passage peacefully and see it as a curious conjuring up of the past. The Agape is but a memory and now the Eucharist is celebrated in church quite apart from ordinary meals. On the contrary since the obligation of receiving Communion fasting has been imposed to prevent any return of the abuses that St Paul pointed out, is not this precisely where we are wrong and what explains the small influence Christians are having in the world, that we see in the Mass a ceremony that ends there? We live like everybody else. We go to church to assist—perhaps very devoutly—at a majestic and mysterious ceremony. That over we return home to lead the same life as before, identical with one's neighbour's, perhaps at heart less christian. We have celebrated the mystery of unity, we have received the Sacrament of brotherly love in the four walls of a church, according to the prescribed and pre-arranged ritual. It has no echo in our real lives. We have sung in chorus, we have approached the holy table with people whose names we may not even know and whose difficulties we do not even seek to discover. And these people, that we have theoretically treated as brethren, do we leave them to return home in their poverty, perhaps in their misery, to get a good breakfast for ourselves?

The reproaches of St Paul nineteen hundred years ago

now, to the christians of Corinth, far from being miles from the point, are they not cuttingly apt? ' When you come together therefore into one place, it is not now to eat the Lord's supper. For everyone taketh before his own supper to eat. And one indeed is hungry and another is drunk.'

Through our own fault there is a risk of Mass becoming as it were robbed of its virtue if we merely make of it a spiritual consolation for selfish and well-nourished christians.

The Eucharist does not really bear fruit, it loses its real significance unless it enkindles in us an immense pity for the world's misery, an insatiable hunger for justice and charity. If our churches are so empty compared with the crowds who remain outside, is it not because we have made a conventional and dead ceremony of what should be the leaven of charity?

In the face of to-day's disbelief can we hear without trembling these words of Christ to his Father: ' That they may be made perfect in one: and the world may know that thou has sent me'. (John 17, 23.)

Chapter VII

LOVE OF GOD

Brotherly Love, fraternal charity, is only the second commandment like to the first, our Saviour said, and it springs from the first. The first commandment is: Thou shalt love the Lord thy God with thy whole heart and thy whole soul and thy whole mind. (Mat. 22, 37.) Such is the gospel text that our *act of charity* translates as: ' My God I love thee with all my heart and above all things, because thou art infinitely lovable '. Without love of our brethren the love of God risks being hypocritical or unreal. But without the love of God love of one's neighbour risks being nothing but natural kindheartedness, philanthropy, even a somewhat contemptuous pity.

This is one of the Christian teachings that people nowadays are most unwilling to admit. If you love me for God's sake, they say, then you do not love me for myself. I do not want this second-hand love. This objection arises from an inadequate idea of God. In fact thence come all objections against God, especially those that concern the reconciling of human liberty with divine omnipotence. God is seen as a creature—someone greater and more powerful than ourselves of course but still of our own category. In that case your love of God is of the same category as the love you have for your fellow man and in loving your brother for God's sake you do not seem to be loving him for his own sake. But remember God is infinitely above all creatures so that he cannot be ranged with them. He is not beside them nor even, strictly speaking, up above them; he envelops them, he contains them.

All that I am, I owe to God. All that I am, is in God. No one can reach me except through God. No one can really love me, without loving God because all that is good in me, all that is deserving of love in me, belongs to God. To make use of a very exact formula of spiritual writers, it is not so much a matter of loving one's neighbour for God's sake as to love him *in God*.

If the first commandment is to love God, one must admit that it is terribly difficult. For this simple reason: we are not angels, pure spirits who live in an invisible world and feed upon incorporeal foods. We have a body which is not a burden or a disguise but which is also *ourselves*, and our most sublime ideas are only brought to birth in us from what we see or what we touch. And if this is true of knowledge, how much more of love? What begets love is the thing nearest to us, the visible thing, the carnal thing. If so few people love God it is because God is invisible. This is very well expressed in the wonderful collect of the fifth Sunday after Pentecost. 'O God, who unto thy lovers hast prepared rewards unseen [that is why it is so difficult to love thee] fix deeply in our hearts thy dart of love [the love of God is something so sublime that it cannot be born of itself, unless God pours it into our hearts] so that ' it concludes ' we may yearn for thee in all and above all, and may come unto those promises of thine which surpass all our yearning.'

When I said we can only love what we see, I was rather hard on human nature. Love is not only concerned with the immediate or carnal things. Many men love, often passionately, invisible realities, such as their country, art, astronomy, mathematics. But if we look into it well, we see that this spiritual love becomes incarnate in material things or in deeds or conduct. One who loves his country sees it in its scenery, its land, its buildings (monuments) in its people and his love is not a sluggish contemplation, it is exercised and developed in the services he renders it often heroically. The man who loves mathematics is not loving an abstract goddess, a kind of allegory of knowledge a colourless statue with vacant eyes, but he finds pleasure in occupying his mind with numbers and consecrates most of his time to this research. Very well, it is the same in proportion with the love of God.

God has commanded us to love him. But he has furnished us with all sorts of visible objects for our love. All kinds of practical means of proving and developing our love for him. With the Jews—who had already been ordered to love God—this love was directed and with what fervour to the Law and the Temple, Jerusalem, the chosen people.

In Christianity, the love of God has become infinitely easier, since God became man so as to become visible and nearer. The Christmas Preface sings just that: ' By the mystery of the Word made flesh a new ray of brightness hath shone upon the eyes of our mind; so that seeing God in visible form we may be drawn by him to the love of things unseen.'

And this incarnate God, Jesus Christ, was not content with showing himself and letting us see God in him. He worked and spent himself for our salvation. He gave us the greatest proof of love which is to lay down one's life for those one loves. Knowing in this way without any doubt that God has loved us infinitely how should we not love him with all our strength?

To that we might object: but it is all a thing of the past ! The Crucifix that shows us so clearly the love of Christ for men, represents a far away event. Christ has returned to heaven. Incarnate no doubt, but he is again invisible.

It is at this point that we come again upon the Eucharist and that we see how it is the sacrament of the love of God.

Through the Eucharist, Jesus, who has gone back to heaven, remains present among us. God remains visible though shrouded in mystery. What is but a memory in the crucifix is a living reality in the Eucharist. For the Christ present under the appearances of consecrated bread is not only or chiefly the Jesus of the crib. It is Jesus crucified and risen again so that we can pass from death to life. As St Paul says ' As often as you shall eat this bread and drink the chalice, you shall show the death of the Lord '. (1 Cor. 11, 26.) Christ instituted this sacrament on the eve of his Passion so as to make of it, all at once, the remembrance and summing up of all his love for us. St John introduces the account of the Last Supper with these words: ' Jesus knowing that he should pass out of this world to the Father, having loved his own who were in the world, he loved them to the end.' (John 13, 1.)

* * *

But it is not enough to say that the Eucharist is the sacrament of the love of God, because it recalls all that God has done for us. If that was all, it might be sufficient to meditate deeply before any ordinary piece of bread. The Eucharist contains the living Christ, and gives him to us to eat. Consequently, it not only represents the love of God, it injects it, so to say, into those who receive it. That is why we are asked not only to look at it, to venerate, to adore the Eucharist, but to eat it. God is there, and we approach as near to him as possible, we absorb him, we unite ourselves to him, we assimilate him. Such a gesture, such conduct, demands love and feeds love. For love knows no distance; it calls for most intimate union and deepest assimilation. The first result of the Eucharist is to increase in us the love of God; as we pray for it in the Collect for the 13th Sunday after Pentecost. ' O almighty and everlasting God, grant us an increase of

faith, hope, and charity; and that we may deserve to
obtain what thou hast promised, make us to love what
thou commandest.'

Of course, all this takes place in the very depths of the
soul. Many first communicants have been deluded by being
told that at the moment when they receive the host, they
will feel their hearts all on fire with the love of God and
they have been deceived and scandalised at experiencing
nothing of the kind. The love of God resides in the depths
where our sensibility is rarely stirred. And that is why the
love of God should always be accompanied with the love
of our brethren. If after communicating, our heart seems
to be insensible it matters little, as long as we are ready
to render efficient service, to devote ourselves, to spread
joy all round us. It is only if we love our fellow men that
we can say that we have love of God in us; ' No man hath
seen God at any time. If we love one another, God abideth
in us: and his charity is perfected in us.' (1 John 4, 3.)

Chapter VIII

DAILY BREAD

In man's heart the love of God is a very frail thing. The difficulties of life, its sorrows, its ugliness, our continually recurring egotism, temptations that come upon us from all directions—from money, from the flesh, from ambition—are for ever weakening in us the love of God and the joy that it brings, and so we slide down into sadness and weariness of life. We drag ourselves along through life. Now, to be exact, the Eucharist is not like baptism, a sacrament received once for all. It is the daily repast. That is one reason why this sacrament makes use of bread.

Holy Scripture contains three types of the Eucharist which show up this aspect of daily sustenance that belongs to bread in our bodily life.

The Jewish people had just been delivered from the inhuman life of slavery and drudgery to which they had been subjected in the land of Egypt. Freed by the blood of the lamb, guided by Moses, they had crossed the Red Sea. They have left the land of bondage. But they are not immediately entering the promised land flowing with milk and honey. First of all they are to wander in the desert for forty years. Progress through the desert is exhausting, discouraging. They are nomads there, without roof, or provisions, uncertain of the morrow. The Jews begin to murmur. Now they are regretting Egypt. Of course they were humiliated and unhappy there, but at least they were well fed. What are they going to eat in this desert? And now at Moses's prayer, God works a miracle. A mysterious substance falls from heaven each morning. At first taken by surprise ('What is that?'—in Hebrew 'Manhou', whence manna got its name) the Hebrews collected this heavenly food, as much as was needed for each family for the day. For it is impossible as well as forbidden to store provisions, to lay in stocks: what is over from the daily food goes bad. And why take precautions, since God is going to send manna every morning without fail? It will never cease to fall until the chosen people have made their entry into the Promised Land that will itself produce all necessary food. This manna had such symbolic import as a testimony of God's gifts and promises that a vessel of it was kept in the Ark of the Covenant with the tables of the Law.

In announcing the coming gift of the Eucharist, our Lord himself said that manna was a figure of it. We can easily see how. The deliverance by the blood of the paschal lamb and the passage through the Red Sea represent baptism which sets us free from sin. But being baptised does not mean entering at once into the Promised Land, into Paradise. We have to go forward slowly and painfully in the desert of this arid life. But while there God feeds us every morning, if we wish it, with a heavenly food which day by day gives us strength and courage: it is the daily bread sent to us by our Father who is in heaven. When we have entered the Promised Land, when we are in heaven, manna will cease to fall, there will be no more Eucharist, for we shall see God face to face and he will be our perfect nourishment without intermediary, without any sacrament.

There is another type of the Eucharist that St Thomas Aquinas has put in its proper place in the Office of Corpus Christi. The prophet Elias had received a difficult mission from God, to resist King Achab to his face. (3 Kings 19, 1-8.) Discouraged and exhausted he fled away and, again in the desert, he lay upon the ground and said to God: 'Lord, take away my soul, for I am no better than my fathers'. And he slept in the shade of a juniper tree. He was awakened by an angel who said to him: 'Arise. Thou hast yet a great way to go,' and the angel showed him a hearth cake and a vessel of water. Strengthened by that food from heaven, Elias set out again and walked forty days as far as the mountain of God, Mount Horeb. This bread is a good type of the Eucharist which restores to us our courage when we are cast down by the contradictions and the apparent foolishness of this world. Sacrament of the love of God, it gives us strength to climb that steep mountain at the top of which we shall find rest and peace in God.

The third episode belongs to the life of Jesus. It is that of the multiplication of the loaves. An enormous crowd has followed Jesus to the great plain where there is nothing to nourish them all. And Jesus says: 'I have pity on the multitude for they have already followed me for three days and they have nothing to eat. If I send them away without food they will faint in the way.' And then he works the miracle of the multiplication of the loaves. He takes this miracle as an opening for the great discourse in which he presents himself as the bread of life and in which he announces the institution of the Eucharist.

In these three cases we see that the Eucharist is not a spiritual luxury, a dainty reserved for the saints, but a substantial food necessary as a remedy for the weaknesses and discouragements of mankind in its weary progress to the Promised Land, towards God.

* * *

We can find still other reasons for the institution of the Eucharist as a sacrament of bread.

Bread is the usual daily food of man. It represents his whole life, his work. To earn his bread means to earn his living—and that still more so as bread is man's proper nourishment. Fruits, meat, might well feed us. But that is also the food of animals. They only need to know how to browse, to gather or to hunt. Whilst the making of bread demands all sorts of operations of which man alone is capable. Sowing, harvesting, thrashing, grinding, kneading, cooking ; all need experience, invention, language to pass on these experiments and inventions. Bread then does not only represent man's life in its most elementary and instructive stage, but also in its most intellectual and most industrious. In offering bread to God we offer him not only his gifts, but his gifts transformed by our intelligence and activity.

Bread represents also the human family. All the Fathers of the Church have remarked that bread is made of a multitude of grains brought to unity by grinding, kneading, and cooking. Again, we might notice that the making of a single morsel of bread represents the working together of a crowd of different trades, farmers, bakers, millers, manufacturers of agricultural implements, mills and bake-houses, providers of motor power, etc. Finally when the bread is on the table the father of the family distributes it to all his guests. These literally communicate by eating the same bread. And so before any consecration, any super-natural intervention, bread suggests union among men. We need not make any great effort to understand that the sacrament of bread, become the sacrament of the body of Christ, is the sacrament of communion, of the community, of the human family of which God is the Father, Jesus the one who gathers them together.

* * *

Finally, wheaten bread has an even higher significance. Jesus himself was compared to a grain of wheat. If it does not die it remains alone. But if it falls to the ground and dies, it brings forth much fruit. (John 12, 24.) Jesus died for us, he was placed in the earth. As the grain comes to life again, in a way, under the form of an ear of corn where the original grain is seen to be multiplied, so Jesus, by dying and rising again from the dead, has given birth to a multitude of brethren like to himself and who in their turn must follow the same law of death, resurrection and multiplication. All the labours that are needed for producing a piece of bread remind us of the labours that were needed for Jesus to give us the Eucharist. He had to humble himself by human birth that he might be bruised in the Passion and die on the Cross and after having been laid in the earth, rise again so as to give us this living and lifegiving bread that we call the Eucharist.[1]

We already see that the sacrament of bread is the sacrament of sacrifice. We shall see it better still when we come to study in the Eucharist the sacrament of the cup, that is to say, the chalice. For the moment let us just notice that the Eucharist is not the sacrament of bread only but also the sacrament of wine. That means that the Eucharist is a complete repast. Man does not only need food, he needs drink. A recent advertising slogan used to say ' a meal without wine is like a day without sunshine '. Bread gives strength; Wine gives joy. (Psalm 103, 15.) Christ willed to revive us completely. In this hard and sad life we not only need strength to do our duty, we also need joy to do it generously and merrily. The Eucharist is not only the sacrament that helps us to work to gain heaven, it is also the sacrament which fills our hearts with thanksgiving towards God.

[1] ' Panis vivus et vitalis '—*Lauda Sion*. ' Panis vivus, vitam praestans homini —*Adoro Te devote*.

CHAPTER IX

THE CHALICE

In Mediterranean countries, just as the basic food is bread so the essential drink is wine. We might say over again in the matter of wine what we have already said about bread : wine is a symbol of unity because it is made of a multitude of pressed grapes and the guests at the same table share the same wine (and this commingling is sometimes shown by the ' healths ' that are drunk and by glasses touched together in friendship).

Besides that, we must notice the supernatural significance of wine. The first concerns not so much the wine as the vine. Many texts of the prophets, notably of Isaiah and Jeremiah (Is. 5, 1-7; Jer. 2, 21-22) and Psalm 79, used the comparison of the vine (that is to say a vineyard) in speaking of the people of God. Israel is the vine that God lovingly tends, that he has transplanted, and that very often disappoints by producing thorns rather than grapes.

In the Gospel many parables show the Kingdom of God as a vineyard where the vine dresser sends his workmen or his sons. (Luke 20, 4-16; Matt. 20, 1-6; 21, 28, 31.) But above all Jesus uses the allegory of the vine at the beginning of his great discourse on the Eucharist to describe the people of God, the Church, under its deepest and most interior aspect: ' I am the vine, you are the branches. Abide in me, and I in you. As the branch cannot bear fruit of itself unless it abide in the vine, so neither can you unless you abide in me.' (John 15, 1-8.) The vine that produces wine, then, all through the Bible, recalls the union of the faithful in one people cherished by God, the Church;

and at the moment of instituting the Eucharist again Jesus makes use of the comparison of the vine to remind us of the necessity of remaining perfectly united to him. All this language is in preparation for the institution of the Eucharist, the sacrament of union with Christ, sacrament of the Church.

If the bread made with crushed grains can in this way recall the Passion, still more wine, which the Bible in many places calls the blood of the grape (Gen. 49, 11: Deut. 32, 14; Eccl. 50, 16; 1 Mac. 6, 34) can make us think of the sacrament of Christ represented and contained in the Eucharist. But here we must follow a new trail that can have no parallel in the matter of bread.

* * *

You may have noticed that while the Eucharist is constituted by two consecrations, two very different formulas are used for these. Whilst the priest says over the bread: ' This is my body,' he does not say over the wine: ' This is my blood,' but ' This is the chalice of my blood '. This particularity is explained by reasons that will help us to enter better into the secrets of the Eucharist. What is in fact the exact value or significance of blood? It might be the effect of a grave accident or a mild haemorrhage, or a surgical operation or of a crime; it might be drawn for a blood stock or a religious sacrifice. We shall see more clearly if that blood is presented to us in a cup or chalice (the two words are synonymous). The chalice prevents the blood from spreading, from being lost, makes it possible to keep hold of it. It shows that it is a question of precious blood. Then the chalice makes it possible to lift up the blood, to make it an offering to God. Finally it makes it possible to pass it round so that everyone can drink. To speak of a chalice of blood is to say that it has a religious value, that it serves as an offering, a sacrifice, a communion.

This is not merely a gratuitous supposition, an ingenious idea. Repeatedly, in Jesus's own language, the chalice means precisely his sacrifice, his Passion. When the mother of James and John, naively asks with ambition that her sons might have first place in his kingdom, Jesus gravely replies, ' Can you drink the chalice that I shall drink?' evidently meaning, before sharing in my glory, are you ready to share my Passion? (Matt. 20, 22.)

In the garden of Olives, we see Jesus on his knees trembling in his human sensitiveness, asking his Father: ' Father if it be possible let this chalice pass from me '. (Matt. 26, 39.) That means that he was trembling before the prospect of the sufferings and degradation of his Passion, and that it meant heroic effort to accept it. But he made this acceptance; and when at the moment of his arrest, Peter, impulsive as usual, tried to defend him and cut off Malchus's ear, Jesus said to him: ' Put up thy sword into the scabbard. The chalice which my Father hath given me, shall I not drink it?' (John 18, 11.) Here again the chalice represents the Passion as accepted and willingly. That is just what makes a sacrifice. Blood is a reminder of bodily suffering. The chalice contains the blood and making it easy to handle represents the submission and love with which that suffering is accepted. The great mystic, St Catherine of Siena, uses this comparison: if a cup-bearer has to offer drink to the king, he does not present him with an empty cup. And he cannot offer him water without the cup. The two must be united: the water and the cup. Water means suffering, the cup means love (*Dialogue* ch. IX). Suffering that is not accepted with love is worthless in the eyes of God. Love that is not proved by suffering risks being more theoretical than real, it is offering an empty cup. What goes to make the sacrifice is the union of suffering and love, it is the offering up of blood under the appearances of wine in the chalice.

* * *

We might go on to analyse the formula of the consecration of the wine ' This is the chalice of my blood of *the new and eternal testament* '. To understand these words, we must bear in mind the history of Israel. What was the testament? In our present day language, the ring that betokens the union of bride and bridegroom. The people of God, Israel, were united to God with a very special link, comparable to marriage. When the prophets reproached Israel for its disobedience, its idolatry, they speak of it as of an adulterous wife, who has been unfaithful towards this mysterious husband, God (notably, Osee, 1-3). This alliance, outlined by Noe (Gen. 9, 10-17), then by Abraham (Gen. 15, 18), concluded by Moses (Ex. 20, 24), has always been ratified by sacrifice. Moses had just received at Sinai, the law of God, the decalogue. He announces it to the people who declare themselves ready to obey. Then Moses concludes the alliance by immolating oxen, whose blood was poured out half upon the people, and half upon the altar, representing God. Then Moses and the Ancients ascended Mount Sinai where ' they saw God '—' they ate and drank '. Such was the ancient alliance, covenant of union and fidelity between Israel and its God. Jesus came to conclude a new alliance, a much more intimate union between God and his people. Like Moses he began by promulgating the law, a new law, which this time is a law of love and freedom. ' A new law I give unto you: that you love one another as I have loved you, that you also love one another.' (John 13, 34.) Afterwards he would seal this new alliance by a sacrifice of bloodshed. But it is no longer the blood of oxen, it is his own blood, really shed on Mount Calvary, and shed sacramentally, this is to say in a mysterious reality, in the sacrifice of the Eucharist.

These words of the consecration of the wine: 'blood of the new and eternal testament', lead us once more to that essential idea that we always find concerning the Eucharist: this does not only bring the individual union of each soul with God, it also brings about the union of all of us in one people and one Church. The Eucharist is the sacrament of unity and of union; the Mass is the sacrifice of the community.

Of course, according to the custom of the Latin Church, the faithful no longer drink from the chalice. But the priest who consecrates drinks from it in their name and that should suffice to remind us that the Mass represents the Passion which gathers all men into one body.

Chapter X

THE SACRIFICE

We have come to one of the greatest difficulties in our study of the Mass. That it is a repast is evident since in it one offers and consumes bread and wine. The Mass however is also and most essentially a sacrifice and that is much more mysterious.

The word sacrifice suggests an offered victim, a bloodshedding. Now whilst we see in the celebration of Mass a table, bread and wine, a plate (the paten), a drinking glass (the chalice), table napkins (altar cloths), we see neither victim, sword, nor bloodshed. Yet it is of faith for Catholics that the Mass is a true sacrifice. This word no longer has a precise meaning for civilized people of the 2oth century. It is no longer used except in figurative language ; and in these expressions the word sacrifice not only means something sad, but what leads us even further astray, something of a loss, a privation. We say, for instance, that in war soldiers have ' sacrificed ' their lives. A merchant will speak of goods sold at a ' sacrifice ', that is to say, goods on which he resigns himself to make no profit. He will also say that ' the management will shrink from no sacrifice in order to satisfy their esteemed customers ' meaning that it will not hesitate to consent to special efforts even to losses, if deserved. Finally, we invite children in devout families to make little ' sacrifices ' which are all translated into hardships or privations, to get up early, not to answer back when scolded, to give up a dainty.

This way of speaking has accustomed us to look upon a

sacrifice as chiefly something painful. Now the Mass is shown to us as a repast—nothing sad about that—or as a feast enhanced with singing, flowers and lights.

The essence of a sacrifice is not a privation, on the contrary it is an enriching. The end of sacrifice, says St Augustine, is to unite us to God so as to preserve for us supreme happiness, supreme riches. We seek to obtain this result by carrying out a visible act which represents and brings about this union with God. For the sacrifice is not carried out on the plane of spiritual realities but on the plane of external signs. To offer a sacrifice is to present an offering to God, sure that God will accept it and will make this human and material reality something sacred. Sacrifice means in fact just exactly ' to make sacred '. How can we be sure that what we offer to God will be accepted and made sacred by him? We are sure of it because we are not offering him any sort of offering of our own choice and in a manner pleasing to ourselves, but precisely the offering that God has decided on and according to the ritual of his own choice.

* * *

These few very simple ideas we can now apply to the Mass and we shall begin to understand what a sacrifice is. The whole of the Mass shows us that here is a question of a mysterious action, directed to God. No one celebrates Mass his own way. It requires an official personage, a priest, dressed in obsolete clothes and this detail already shows that it is not a question of an everyday or utilitarian act. The gestures and words of this priest are not spontaneous but minutely regulated by a ceremonial. The offerings even are not left to our free choice. They are bread and wine, because our Lord commanded us to celebrate the sacrifice as he did, taking bread and wine at the Last Supper. We place these offerings upon an altar, that is to say not on an ordinary table, but on a consecrated stone where we are sure of meeting God, where we are sure that God will come in some way to receive them. Better still, the priest *consecrates* these offerings making of them something truly sacred since they become the body and blood of Jesus Christ, who is God.   Finally we eat and drink this bread, the body and blood of Jesus Christ so much so that it is impossible to unite oneself more truly to God than in assimilating the divine humanity of Christ.

But, you will say, how can we speak of sacrifice where no flesh is immolated, no blood shed?

To become united to God, which is the aim of sacrifice, we must not overlook certain obstacles. First of all our egotism: we always have a tendency to make ourselves the centre of the world, to stand up against God. To be more precise, we are separated from God by sin. The obstacles cannot be removed except by obedience which makes up for sin's rebellion, and by the love that breaks down the crust of egoism. Jesus overcame these obstacles by his great, unique sacrifice of the Cross, where his cruel death, accepted in love and obedience, made reparation for the ruin caused by man's sin and selfishness. In suffering and dying on the cross Jesus offered himself to his Father in a definite and visible way and by so doing he reunited to his Father humanity that had been separated from him by sin. So he opened for man the way of happiness. That is the end of sacrifice. Death, bloodshed, immolation were but the means.

* * *

Because he was perfectly pure and holy, Jesus alone could offer this sacrifice. But he wished us to have a share in it, to sacrifice ourselves with him. As it is not possible for us to renew the sacrifice of Calvary, offered once for all, Jesus has found a means of renewing this sacrifice truly but under another form. On the eve of his death, he took bread and wine, consecrated them so that they became his immolated body and blood and commanded us to take up again this mysterious sacrifice. When we celebrate Mass, we do again what Jesus did at the Last Supper. We do not do again what he did upon the cross. We do not put him to death once more—happily—but we render present on the altar the sacrifice of his body and blood, in such a way that we renew the offering that redeemed mankind. As the Secret says on the ninth Sunday after Pentecost ' As often as the memory of this victim is kept (by the Mass), is the work of our redemption (accomplished once for all on the cross) renewed '. Such is the great mystery of the Mass: it is at once both a memorial (do this in remembrance of me) and a new realisation of the work of Redemption.

* * *

To understand better that the Mass, without violence, without immolation, is a sacrifice, we must see how the Last Supper is itself a sacrifice, since the Mass consists in literally reproducing the Last Supper, so well that by it, it reproduces but in different language, the Cross itself.

How is the Last Supper a sacrifice? First of all because it is a Pasch. Now the Pasch is a sacrifice under the form of a meal. When, prescribes Exodus, you renew the Paschal meal, and your children ask you ' What is the meaning of this service?' you will answer ' It is the *victim* of the passage of the Lord.' (Ex. 12, 26.)

One might ask, it is true, if Jesus really celebrated the Pasch with his disciples, for they ate the Last Supper on Thursday evening. It certainly seems indeed from reading St John that the Pasch was celebrated on the Friday evening. In fact he calls the Friday the ' parasceve ' (John 19; 14, 31, 42) that means in preparation for the Pasch; the Jews were unwilling to enter into Pilate's praetorium

on the Friday ' because it was the parasceve ', so as to
be able to eat the Pasch; the crucified were taken down
so that they would not remain on the cross during the
Sabbath for (the eve) was the Parasceve.

Yet the synoptic evangelists declare formally that the
repast of Thursday evening was a paschal meal. (Matt.
26, 17-9; Mark 14, 12-4; Luke 22, 7-8, 11, 13, 15.)
In every case, for them as for St John, the Parasceve was
on the Friday. (Matt. 27, 62; Mark 15, 42; Luke 23, 54.)
We may suppose then that the official day of the Pasch fell
that year upon a Saturday and that the Jews gathered in
Jerusalem were beginning its celebration on the Friday
evening ; but that the people from Provincial towns like
Jesus and his disciples who were Galileans, could anticipate
the paschal meal on the Thursday evening (besides the
family from whom Jesus borrowed the supper room would
need it to celebrate their own paschal meal).

Whatever may be the problem of exegesis and the
hypothetical solution that can be proposed for it, one thing
is certain and that is what interests us; for the Synoptics
who alone record the institution of the Eucharist, this is a
Pasch, a new Pasch. For St John, Jesus Christ crucified is
the Paschal Lamb. (John 19, 36.) These things were done
(Jesus's legs were not broken as had been done to the
two thieves) that the scripture might be fulfilled: ' you
shall not break a bone of him ': which is a ritual prescrip-
tion concerning the Paschal Lamb. (Ex. 12, 46.)

From these two affirmations, all the more striking as
they are difficult to reconcile, we can then deduce the deep
identity of the Last Supper and the cross as fulfilling in both
cases the figurative Pasch of the ancient covenant. Whatever
the ritual celebrated at the Last Supper this was indeed a
Pasch and therefore a sacrifice like the cross.

St John himself links up the Last Supper with the Pasch

since he begins the account of what passed at the Cenacle with this characteristic phrase ' Before the festival day of the Pasch, Jesus knowing that *his hour was come* that he *should pass out of this world to the Father*; having loved his own who were in the world, he loved them to the end.' (John 13, 1.) For St John Jesus's hour was the carrying out of the death and resurrection mystery. (John 2, 4; 5, 25, 28; 12, 23, 27; 17, 1). And the word Pasch means precisely Passage. (Ex. 12, 11.)

If St John does not relate the actual institution of the Eucharist, he relates the washing of the feet of which the significance is sacrificial. First of all because that act has the same end as the sacrifice; unity in charity. Then because there Jesus adopts the position of a servant which recalls the servant of Jahweh (Isa. 53) put to death for the sins of his people. This comparison becomes clear if we read the parallel discourse in the Synoptics. ' Even as the Son of Man is not come to be ministered unto but to minister and to give his life a redemption for many .' (Matt. 20, 28; Mark 10, 45: cf. Isaiah 53, 4-12.)

This account of the beginning of the Last Supper is connected with the treason of Judas, whom Jesus sends away from the Cenacle to carry out his business ' quickly ', and so the Last Supper involves and in a way opens up the Passion. (John 13, 12, 21-30; Matt. 26, 21-24; Luke 22, 21-3.) Besides in the Holy Week liturgy what we call the Passion always includes this determining episode which took place at the Cenacle.

In the institution of the Eucharist itself we have already indicated the sacrificial meaning of the words: For this is my body *given for you* (Luke 22, 19; cf 1 Cor. 11, 24), and of the whole formula for the consecration of the chalice (see above chap.: IX *The Chalice*).

As to the words that follow the institution in St John

(what we call 'the discourse of the Last Supper' chaps. 14-17) they show the sacrificial value of the Eucharist. There is no question there of real presence, nor of immolation, nor of the connection between the Last Supper and the Cross. But the general theme is that of the end and fruits of sacrifice: charity, unity, the gathering together in one body. Chapter 17 in particular is justly called 'the sacerdotal prayer' which means sacrificial and it has been often noticed that its style as well as its contents recalls in a striking way the most ancient anaphora (or liturgical prayers that surround the consecration).

One last argument, more theological than scriptural, greatly increases the deep unity of the Cross, the Last Supper and the Mass, and so the sacrificial character of the last two. The Cross is a unique and perfect sacrifice because the same person is both priest and victim in it. Ordinary sacrifices require a priest, as religious and deliberate as possible, and a victim as pure and precious as possible but yet distinct; so much so that the priest offers but does not offer himself; the victim is immolated but involuntarily and unknowingly. On the Cross, on the contrary, the same one is the perfectly holy victim and the perfectly deliberate priest. No one can doubt that Jesus is the victim. If the Cross is not just one fact among others, the result of a legal error, but a sacrifice, the priest is Jesus who is perfectly his own master.[1]

On the Cross Jesus is both priest and victim in person,

---

[1] This really requires much developing; we see how Jesus did not let himself be taken but lays down his life voluntarily (John 10, 18); how he went up to Jerusalem of his own free will knowing what awaited him there; how he presented himself and declared his identity to those who came to arrest him; how he answered Caiphas beyond the question asked of him, by the very words that would condemn him; how he was silent or spoke with authority before Herod or Pilate; how on the Cross he speaks as a sovereign, without complaining, etc. All this is confirmed by the fact that he rises again of his own power, as he had foretold.

in his physical and natural state. Equally at the Last Supper Jesus is priest and victim. But if he is priest in person he is victim sacramentally, under the species of bread and wine (so that he is not sacrificed nor is his blood shed except sacramentally). Finally in the Mass, the same Jesus is still at the same time priest and victim. Victim sacramentally exactly as at the Last Supper; and priest sacramentally too in so far as the words of consecration are pronounced by a human priest who takes his place to the extent of saying: This is *my* body.

All this confirms that the immolation of the Mass is a true immolation, although *representative* in so far as the Mass reproduces the Last Supper which in its turn represents and involves the entire Cross.

* * *

So the Mass translates into sacramental language the redeeming quality that is comprised in the Cross, and makes it possible to renew it. To what purpose? Was not the sacrifice of Christ on the Cross sufficient to save the whole world? Doubtless, but Christ willed us to cooperate in our salvation. He did not mean us to be saved without doing something ourselves. He devised the Eucharist so that we could offer *our* sacrifice in union with *his* sacrifice. The offering of bread and wine is not only meant to renew Christ's sacrifice but to join our own to it. As St Augustine said, God who created us without our help has not willed to save us without our help. That is why the Church not only asks us to assist at Mass as at a sacrifice taking place at a distance of which we are merely spectators and inert beneficiaries, it asks us to take part in it, that is to say to unite ourselves to it, to offer ourselves up with Christ, to sacrifice ourselves with him, and to join ourselves to him by communion. Otherwise there would be no need for us

to go to Mass; it would not even be any use celebrating
Mass. It would suffice for Christians to remember from time
to time that formerly, a long time ago, Jesus died for them,
and so let themselves be saved while doing nothing towards
it.

* * *

To offer oneself up with Christ; to immolate oneself
with him does that mean we are to go up to Calvary and
shed our blood? No, certainly. It means that we should
take part in the Mass, in an intelligent and active way, that
we should try to understand what the priest is doing,
express our union with him and among ourselves by our
answers, our singing, our postures. It means above all that
we should not content ourselves with going to Mass as a
ceremony that has no influence on our lives but that there
we resolve, and there we draw strength, to destroy all
that is opposed to our union with God, and to develop all
that deepens that union, that is to say first and above all,
charity, our devotedness to God and our fellow men. The
Mass, the Eucharist, is the sacrament of sacrifice which
means, finally, of our deification by the generous gift of
ourselves.

CHAPTER XI

CHRIST'S RESURRECTION

The Mass is the memorial of the death of our Lord, we know, but we must not forget that it is at the same time the sacrament of the resurrection. That implies two things that are distinct and yet connected, both of which are important: first of all that Christ is present in the Eucharist as the risen Christ; further that we receive the Eucharist as a pledge of our own resurrection.

First of all, Christ present in the Eucharist is the risen Christ. We cannot separate the dead Christ from the risen Christ. If Christ died for us, he has proved to us his love in that way: ' No one hath greater love than to give his life for his friends '. But that death is sterile unless it is followed by the resurrection. Remember the state of prostration of the apostles who had seen Christ die and who did not believe in his resurrection. Remember the discouragement of the pilgrims to Emmaus who had seen all their hopes vanish in the anguish of Calvary. Years later St Paul would say; ' If Christ be not risen again, your faith is vain . . . we are of all men most miserable '. (1 Cor. 15, 17, 19.) Christ's death without his resurrection was a terrible blow that he had undergone in spite of himself. Death followed by resurrection is a voluntary sacrifice and a victory.

We must not look upon the resurrection as a sort of unimportant appendix, a sort of guarantee that the Passion had not been useless. Many present day Christians would readily attach more importance to Good Friday than to Easter Sunday. The first Apostles did not think so. The great theme of their preaching was this victorious declaration : ' Christ is risen '. Of course that implies that he had died first. But the two mysteries of death and resurrection are only one, and that one is the fundamental mystery of Christianity, the mystery of Easter. St John tells us that on Maundy Thursday Jesus knew that the hour had come when he must pass from this world to his Father. This *passage* is just exactly what the mystery of Easter consists of, for the Pasch or Passover means *passage*. All passing supposes two things, a departure and an arrival. In Christ's passover, the departure is death by which he left this world in sorrow, the arrival is the resurrection completed by the Ascension by which he is assured a glorious return to his Father. The mystery of our salvation is the mystery of Easter made up, if we may say so, of two aspects that we can distinguish but not separate, the humiliating, sorrowful, purifying aspect of the Passion and death and the glorious, joyful, and prolific aspect of the Resurrection. The Eucharist contains the whole mystery of our salvation put at our disposal every day. It contains the mystery in its actual, concrete manner because it substantially contains Christ : Christ present in the Eucharist is then the dead and risen Christ at the same time.

* * *

Immediately an objection comes to mind : the words of consecration which bring to pass the real presence of Christ in the Eucharist make no allusion to his resurrection and seem only to consider his death and passion, in so far as they concern the body and blood of Christ successively. For separation of body and blood can only happen in someone subjected to violent death.

We can make two answers to this objection. We can repeat what we have just said, that the death of Christ cannot really be separated from the resurrection—if the

Eucharist gave us nothing but a dead Christ it would not comprise the whole mystery of our salvation.

There is another and more precise answer. The consecration renders present in the Eucharist the body and blood of Christ as they actually exist. The priest in fact says in the present tense: This *is* my body. This *is* the chalice of my blood. Now in actual fact Christ is in heaven, risen, living and glorious. The words of consecration must then render present in the Eucharist, Christ living, risen and glorious. They designate and produce directly either the body alone or the blood alone. But since there is question of a living body, the body in becoming present under the appearance of bread brings the blood with it. For this reason the Western Church has allowed the communion of the precious blood to drop out for the faithful : in receiving the body of Christ only, under the appearance of bread, the communicant receives the whole Christ, blood, soul and divinity.

We have just brought forward a liturgical argument. No other is so valuable where the sacraments are concerned. The best theological demonstration is not so important as an established custom of the Church an almost unconscious, I might say, instinctive custom surrounding the declaration of a truth. The fact that for centuries, in the West, the faithful have communicated in the body of Christ alone shows that Christ present in the Eucharist is the living and risen Christ.

Here are some further proofs in the liturgical order. Immediately after the consecration, the priest says a very important and very beautiful prayer found in all liturgies, the *Unde et memores* which is called the ' anamnesis ' that is to say the prayer of remembrance. After repeating the words of Christ ' As often as ye shall do these things ye shall do them in remembrance of me ', the priest goes on

' Wherefore, O Lord, we thy servants as also thy holy people calling to mind the blessed Passion of the same Christ thy Son, our Lord, and also his blessed resurrection from hell and his glorious ascension into heaven, offer unto thy most excellent Majesty . . . a perfect victim.' If we believe in this prayer every Mass renders present on the altar all the mysteries of Christ as well as the Passion.

That is why the Church celebrates feasts of every kind by the Mass and the Eucharistic consecration. Whether it is Easter, Christmas or the Ascension, Mass is celebrated, always the Mass, because the Mass contains the living Christ in every mystery that bears the glorious mark of his death. The celebrating of Mass all through the christian year with its various feasts also proves that the Eucharist makes and preserves to us the living and risen Christ. For the rest, let us not forget that the first of all these feasts in importance as well as in date is the feast of Easter, the feast of Christ's death and resurrection. The earliest Christians, so it seems, knew no other feast, to-day it still remains the ' Solemnity of Solemnities ', it was little by little that special feasts such as Christmas and the Ascension became distinct. The primary object of our faith, the centre and apex of the Christian mystery is Christ who died and rose again.

After the ceremony of the breaking of bread, much reduced at the present day, the priest lets a fragment of his host drop into the chalice. We do not know the exact origin of this gesture. Perhaps they had to soften the consecrated bread that had been kept from the previous Mass and that had hardened being unleavened bread. This ritual made sure of a unity among all Masses in time just as the rite of *fermentum* mentioned above assured unity of space in all Masses. Whatever may be the origin of this rite we are allowed to see in this reuniting of the body and blood of Christ a sign reminding us that Christ present and immolated on the altar is at the same time the living and risen Christ, since their separate consecration signified his death.

Finally the Christians of old communicated standing. Eastern Christians have remained faithful to this custom. It is meant to show that Communion unites us to the risen Christ and is the pledge of our resurrection as we are soon to see.

In any case from now on, we see that the often tearful and sentimental notion that many have of the Eucharist needs revising. Our religion is not only a religion of memories of the past, brooding sadly over a death. It is a religion of life, hope, conquest, all directed towards life and resurrection. The Eucharist which is the centre and the sun of our Catholicism is not, and cannot be, the sacrament of death, nor a sacrifice of bloodshed considered in themselves. These are the inevitable ways and means that lead to the radiant glory of the resurrection. It is not for nothing that the feast of the Eucharist, called in France ' la Fête-Dieu '—the God-Feast, makes so much of the Alleluia and that we sing in the Lauda Sion that it is ' a living and life giving bread ' (panis vivus et vitalis). How should we receive life if we were communicating with death?

Chapter XII

OUR OWN RESURRECTION

If the Eucharist contains the risen Christ, if it is the Easter Sacrament its effect should be to cause us also to rise again. For the Eucharist likens us to Christ. That is a general law: All nourishment leads to an assimilation. But whilst ordinary foodstuffs are assimilated to our person (by eating it I do this beef or that lettuce the honour of entering into the substance of my human body) so that the lower is assimilated to the higher: here, then, the one eating is assimilated to the one eaten. St Augustine expressed this in a few words: ' I am the food of the great,' he makes Christ say, ' eat me and I shall not be changed into you but you will be changed into me '. By eating the risen Christ we must ourselves become risen, to his image and under his direct influence.

Jesus himself made this clear in his great discourse on the bread of life that he delivered after the multiplication of the loaves, to announce the institution of the Eucharist. ' Amen, Amen, I say to you he that believeth in me hath everlasting life. I am the bread of life. Your fathers did eat manna in the desert and are dead. This is the bread which cometh down from heaven: that if any man eat of it he may not die. I am the living bread which came down from heaven, if any man eat of this bread he shall live for ever. And the bread that I will give is my flesh for the life of the world.' (John 6, 47-52.) A little further on Jesus takes up the same declarations more forcefully and more precisely. ' Amen, Amen, I say to you except you eat the flesh of the Son of Man and drink his blood you shall not have life in you. He that eateth my flesh and drinketh my blood hath everlasting life: and I will raise him up on the last day . . . This is the bread that came down from heaven. Not as your fathers did eat manna and are dead (that is to say after eating this bread from heaven, the manna) he that eateth this bread shall live for ever.' (John 6, 55-9.)

Now notice the passage that explains this astonishing statement. ' My flesh is meat indeed: and my blood is drink indeed. He that eateth my flesh and drinketh my blood abideth in me and I in him. As the living Father hath sent me and I live by the Father, so he that eateth me, the same also shall live by me.' (John 6, 56-8.)

The argument is very simple. The body of Christ is really a food. The object of food is to give life. The life of Christ is a divine life, the very life of his heavenly Father. Consequently in absorbing this true nourishment that the body of Christ is, we unite ourselves to his life which is the life of God, an eternal life.

We see here with what a virile and keen spirit the Christian should go to Mass to find there relief, solace, strength against temptation, and in general against all the miseries and wear and tear of human life. It is not because he finds there a more or less emotional feeling; it is because he enters into mysterious but absolutely real communication with the life of Christ, with the divine life which passes into him and becomes his own life.

* * *

There is in the Catholic Church a venerable institution almost forgotten in our days, which strikingly shows up the value of the Eucharist as a sacrament of eternal life and resurrection. This is Holy Viaticum. The word means holy communion administered to the dying. We have developed a habit of looking upon Extreme Unction as the sacrament of the dying. Really it is the anointing of the sick and that is its true name, much more than the unfortunate and incxact expression, ' extreme unction '. The proof of this is that it is forbidden to give extreme unction to a man condemned to death, to soldiers who are about to make a very dangerous assault, to one who is going to undergo a serious operation. These are not sick people and the text of prayers for the anointing of the sick never mentions death, but always sickness or recovery. Hence it is illogical, though too frequently done, to administer this sacrament to those who are at the last extremity.

There is a sacrament of the dying whether they are ill or not, and that is the Eucharist given as *Viaticum*, from a word meaning provision for a journey. At the moment of undertaking the great journey and passing into immortality, the Christian should carry away with him the ' holy much needed Viaticum ' as the ancients called it. The reception of Viaticum is obligatory for the dying. Also many of the usual rules are dispensed with in these circumstances. No sort of fast is required and anyone who has already communicated can and ought to receive Viaticum the same day. A priest who is not fasting can and ought to say Mass, if necessary, so as to secure Viaticum for a dying person.

The early Christians held so strongly to the Viaticum that they used to keep the Eucharist in their houses, it was because of the need of being able to give Viaticum to the dying that the custom was introduced of reserving the Eucharist apart from the Mass. The early Christians even had such faith in the efficacy of Viaticum that action had to be taken against a pretty frequent abuse which consisted of giving Communion to the dead. All this shows how the Eucharist is the sacrament of the immortality, not only of the soul, but also of the body which will itself arise again on the Last Day, just as Christ rose again, the Christ whose living flesh it has eaten throughout its mortal life.

I have spoken of rising again at the Last Day. We know quite well in fact, that if the Eucharist is the sacrament of our resurrection if it makes risen bodies of us, we are not risen again yet. We are only risen in hope. We should not let ourselves think of this hope as of a vague probability. It is a certainty because Christ our head, whose members we are, is already risen. This is what made St Paul say with confident boldness: ' And hath raised us up together and hath made us sit together in the heavenly places through Christ Jesus.' (Eph. 2, 6.) In fact by baptism our resurrection is achieved in advance.

When the priest receives at the church door a candidate for baptism he puts to him the following questions ' What do you ask of the Church of God?'—' Faith ' (that is to say the sacrament of faith, baptism)—' And what does faith give you?'—'Eternal life '. It is not put into the future tense, what will it give you? but rather in the present ' What does it give you? ' Christ has told us, ' He that believeth in me, *hath* life everlasting '. (John 3, 36, cf. 5, 24.)

* * *

If this risen life, if this eternal life, has already been acquired by baptism, because it incorporates us into Christ dead and risen again, we must also gain this eternal life by our daily life. This will be the work of the Eucharist. In fact this is a sacrament that requires something else besides a respectful and even pious reception: a will to grow in the Christian life, to progress in the love of God and our brethren. Children eat to grow ; adults it is true only eat to keep up their strength. But from the spiritual point of view we are always children here below, we shall only be adults in heaven. As long as we live on this earth we must grow, we must advance. The sacrament of this unlimited progress is the Eucharist. That is why whilst

other sacraments are only given once, or in certain circumstances: when we have sinned, when we are ill, when we
establish a home the Eucharist is the daily bread, the
sacrament that we must go and receive indefinitely. What
should regulate the frequency of our communions is not
our pleasure: the Eucharist is not a spiritual dainty; it is
not our perfection: the Eucharist is not a reward. It is the
desire and above all the need that we have to grow in
strength, in virtue, and first of all in the chief of all virtues,
charity, it is therefore a sacrament that makes us look
upwards and onwards. It is not meant for us if we are deter-
mined to remain stationary.

The prayers that are said after the Communion, and that
are therefore called post-communions, usually run upon
this theme: Lord we have taken part in your mysteries,
we have received your body. Grant that this may not
remain a mere ceremony but that it will transform our
lives; so that, advancing step by step, we may reach even
to heaven of which this sacrament of your dead and risen
body gives us not only a promise, but a foretaste and a
beginning.

Chapter XIII

MEMORIAL OF TIMES TO COME

The Christian is not a man of the past but a man of the future. He is awaiting, he is all straining towards the future world. Christians of to-day have lost this essential dimension of their faith. Yet they continue to sing every Sunday the Nicene Creed where it holds such a high place. We proclaim our faith in Christ who is not only born of the Virgin Mary and suffered under Pontius Pilate—events dated in history, in the past—but who, once risen again, ' ascended into heaven, seated at the right hand of the Father, whence he shall come again to judge the living and the dead, and his kingdom shall have no end.'

After having professed our faith in Christ as judge at the end of time, the *Credo* in its third part professes faith in the Holy Ghost and his work; the life of the Church that he animates. It ends with this double and unique declaration on the end or apotheosis of the life of the Church in the Spirit. ' I await the resurrection of the dead and the life of the world to come. Amen.'

In the Gospel, this belief in Christ's return and in the time to come is constantly manifested. Chapters 24 & 25 of St Matthew are entirely occupied with it. The Common of Saints in the Missal continually recalls the parable of the servants, some of whom sleep while others watch whilst their master has gone on a journey; some are surprised by the master's unexpected return, coming at midnight like a thief, others welcome him with joy; and the parable of the virgins is another warning of the Last Judgement, when the spouse of the Church, the Son of Man, will come again on the clouds, as the prophets had foretold, notably Daniel (Ch. 7, 13-4), and as Jesus solemnly declared before Caiphas so that they could say that he had died for having professed his title of Supreme Judge, at the end of time. (Matt. 27, 64.)

In the Apostles' preachings and epistles we find this constant conviction. Of course St Peter's Second Epistle, the two Epistles of St Paul to the Thessalonians, especially the second, contend against popular errors about the proximity of this return. They warn the faithful against a passive interpretation of this expectancy which might lead to a sort of fatalism or quietism. They insist no less on the ontological, if not chronological, proximity of Christ's return, on the duty of actively expecting it, preparing for it, hastening it. The Apostles speak incessantly of the ' day of the Lord ', taking up again into Christian use an expression of the prophets and Psalms that describes the terrible judgment of Yahweh always shown as imminent.

The great prayer of the early Christians is; ' Come Lord Jesus,' in Aramaic ' Maran atha ', which is found in the conclusion not only of the 1st Epistle to the Corinthians, but also of the Apocalypse and therefore of the whole Bible.

* * *

If the expectation of the day of the Lord, if this last day doctrine is an essential element of our faith and our life, why should it be absent from the Mass?

The Mass, however, is our Lord's memorial. To say remembrance or memorial is, it seems, to speak of recalling the past. Has our Mass no other use than to revive in us the memory of Jesus's benefits? If we hold to that, we shall be joining Calvin, for whom the ' Lord's Supper ' is a mere remembrance, an empty sign, only meant to refresh our memories or warm up our piety. The Mass is endowed with a realism that is quite different, with a plentitude that is quite other. When we say that the words of consecration bring about the 'real presence' we must take that expression in every sense of the word and not restrict it to a sort of limited and static presence of the person of Jesus under the appearances of bread and wine. There is a *presence* that is to say something actual at the *present time*; and a *real* presence, that is to say a presence of the whole reality of the mysteries of Christ, living in his Church and causing his Church to live. This complete meaning, that we shall develop, is not opposed to the current sense of the expression 'real presence'; it gives it its whole meaning which is immense.

When we sing, after the elevation, a motet to the Blessed Sacrament, we make the mistake of stopping at the 'real presence' taken in a limited sense, whereas the liturgical prayers that follow the consecration are endowed with quite a different force and disclose quite different boundaries.

As he puts down the chalice, the priest repeats the words of Jesus 'Do this in memory of me' in the Greek of our Gospels 'Eis ten emon anamnesin' whence we get the word *anamnesis*.

He replies, like an echo, with the Church's answer carrying out and interpreting this order: '*Unde et memores*'. 'Wherefore O Lord (this prayer is addressed to the Father) we thy servants (the celebrant with his assistants), as also thy holy people (the congregation of baptised souls)—what and whom are we remembering? The text goes on: '*Ejusdem Filii tui Domini nostri beatae Passionis*'. It is not a question of the stationary and timeless person of Christ, of a sort of abstract Christ, as outside of the history of salvation, but of his mysteries that are to be solemnly enumerated.

'*Beatae Passionis*,' his blessed Passion. Not sorrowful; it was that in its historical and unique reality. But here, the memory, the anamnesis, is not a mere memory referring to the historic event. It is far more: a re-presentation, a sacramental realisation, of the mystery. The Mass renders present the Passion in its intent, in its fruits, in its value as a voluntary sacrifice, in its efficacious ' mystery ', which makes us blessed. St Augustine says the sacrifice is ' an act ' . . . by which we are united to God in such a way as to be truly blessed.

' *Necnon et ab inferis resurrectionis.*' His resurrection from hell, which completes and sanctions the sacrifice. Here again we are not merely referring to the past when Christ rose once and for all, to a moment of time. Christ made present in the Eucharist *is* the risen Christ. We have settled that point above.

' *Sed et in coelis gloriosae ascensionis* and glorious ascension into heaven.' The Ascension too as an historical event, belongs to the past, but the Eucharist makes it present as a lasting and actual mystery, full of sanctifying realness. The Eucharistic Christ is the Christ of to-day, seated at the right hand of the Father.

So the Eucharist contains the whole mystery of redemption, very far from limiting itself to the sole commemoration of the Passion. We see here how radically false in principle—and so often ridiculous in detail—are the allegorical explanations of the Mass which we have multiplied from the middle ages to our own day. They suppose that the Mass represents Christ's Passion after the manner of a succession of tableaux. Each rite, instead of being studied in its natural setting in the liturgy, is isolated and compared with some feature of the Passion. As these comparisons are absolutely arbitrary and artificial, so they vary or contradict each other according to their authors. In this way the *Lavabo* for some represents the washing of the feet before the Last Supper and for others Pilate's washing of his hands after the condemnation of Jesus. Whatever may be the details, what is most deplorable in these interpretations is that they impoverish the Mass reducing it to a sort of mimed riddle or spiritless allegory, all referring to a historic past, whereas it is a mystery that transcends all time and which therefore includes the past but by rendering it present; as a mystery it also makes present the whole future of which the past contained the germ and the promise.

We can take again the three basic mysteries enumerated in the *Unde et memores* so as to try and consider how they include the future.

'The blessed Passion' is the dawn of a new time, the inauguration of the end of time. It closes the era of sin to open that of holiness. Holy Church, the new people, the new Jerusalem are born from the open side of Jesus whence water and blood spring up 'to eternal life'. Now mankind possesses this treasure of holiness, sufficient to save all men. Henceforth heaven is opened not only because the obstacles that barred the entrance have been abolished, but also more positively, because mankind, until the end of time and even in heaven, will have nothing more to do than make use of this inexhaustible capital, the sacrifice of Jesus. A historic episode of the Passion is very characteristic here. Jesus on the cross said to the repentant thief: 'Amen, I say to thee, to-day thou shalt be with me in paradise.' (Luke 23, 43.) One might have asked what *to-day* means. Will the thief be in paradise before Jesus who will not enter there for forty days, at his ascension? That is a false problem. That to-day does not mean a day of twenty-four hours. We are not concerned with earthly time measurements, but with that of the economy of salvation. That 'to-day' is the day that our Lord inaugurated by his blessed Passion, the day that came after the long watching and preparing and waiting of the old alliance, and will end in judgment when the day of the Lord will coincide with eternal life. Jesus exactly answers the thief's prayer: Jesus remember me when thou shalt come into the splendour of thy kingdom. Jesus teaches him that between his crucifixion and his return, there is no real interval, in spite of appearances.

The resurrection is not only an event in the personal life of Jesus. Jesus being the head of humanity and the first born of a multitude of brethren, his resurrection is the beginning of ours, which will not be entirely realised until ' the resurrection of the body ' at the day of judgment. Such is the argument that supports all St Paul's reasoning in chapter the 15th of his 1st epistle to the Corinthians: if Christ has risen again we shall all rise again because our resurrection is contained in his own, that is why he rises again on the first day of the week which is also the eighth day: his resurrection is the beginning of a new creation, of a new world succeeding and replacing the old. Positive economy is succeeding provisional economy.

The *Unde et memores* does not only say: the resurrection of Christ, it states precisely his resurrection from hell, *ab inferis*. The expression is eloquent. Jesus rises again after sinking into the mysterious depths where the just men of the Old Testament were awaiting him. He went to open and empty ' their prison ' (1 Peter 3, 19) because the law of waiting and captivity was at an end.

He positively destroyed this captivity by his glorious *Ascension into heaven*. ' Wherefore he saith: Ascending on high he led captivity captive; he gave gifts to men. Now that he ascended, what is it but because he also descended first into the lower parts of the earth? He that descended is the same that ascended above all the heavens, that he might fill all things.' (Eph. 4, 8-10 quoting Ps. 67, 19.)

The ascension through which the humanity of Jesus begins its glorious reign at the right hand of the Father and introduces our humanity into heaven, already proclaims Christ's glorious return as the world's judge. As the angels said to the Apostles: ' Ye men of Galilee why stand you looking up to heaven? This Jesus who is taken up from you into heaven shall so come as you have seen him going into heaven.' (Acts 1, 11.)

Other liturgies, less restrained than our Roman Rite, have been able to draw out this enumeration of the ' anamnesis ', to join to it for example mention of the parousia or Second Coming of Christ. The three mysteries of our *Unde et memores* really imply the second coming. In making a ' remembrance ' of the Passion, Resurrection and Ascension, the Eucharist renders the mysteries of the future world present in the sacrament. By doing so, it prepares for and inaugurates a future world where the Eucharist itself will disappear, because that future world will be one of absolute reality where not only the empty types of the Old Covenant, but even the sacramental signs, although fully real, of the New Covenant will vanish away, together with faith and hope. St Paul said so in these few words, ' For as often as you shall eat this bread and drink the chalice you shall show the death of the Lord *until he come.*' (1 Cor. 11, 26.) Christ's return by establishing the rule of unveiled reality, of face to face vision and union without intermediary, will abolish the Eucharist not in itself but in its sacramental state, there will be no more Pasch, or passing, because the goal will have been reached and possessed. The manna prefigured this economy: it fell each day during the journey through the desert which was like our journey through life. It ceased to fall when the promised land was reached: this promised land with its natural fertility made the law of daily bread obsolete, by making the chosen people enter into the realm of eternal day and full possession.

* * *

The *anamnesis* and the anticipation of glory are again detailed in the two prayers that follow:

The prayer *Supra quae* connects the eucharistic sacrifice with those of the times of the promise. Abel is a figure of Christ because he is the just one who offers a sacrifice pleasing to God and who consummates it with his blood, shed by his brother Cain. Abraham is a foreshowing of the Father putting his Son to death. As is said in the preface for the consecration of an altar: the Son is offered up and the Lamb is sacrificed. Abraham's sacrifice again foreshadows our own because it is pleasing to God by virtue of the obedience and faith that inspires it. Finally Melchisedech ' high-priest ' of the supreme God, who offers bread and wine prefigures so well the priesthood of Christ that Christ is called ' a priest for ever according to the order of Melchisedech.' (Gen. 14, 18, 20; Ps. 109, 4; Heb. 5, 6; 6, 20; 7, 17.) Of course all these figurative sacrifices are of little substantial value compared to the eucharistic sacrifice. What prevents the sacrifice from being quite unseemly is that Christ's sacrifice, though incomparable in itself, at the Mass becomes *our* sacrifice. The comparison holds good especially between the sentiments that animated Abel, Abraham and Melchisedech and those that should animate ourselves. A sacrifice is not only of value according to the victim offered up but according to the intention of those who offer. If they were animated by faith and religion were they not also urged by hope for times to come? Were their sacrifices not an augury of the one true sacrifice and did they not participate in its holiness in advance?

The prayer *Supplices* is concerned only with the future.

It binds together the present sacrifice accomplished at the altar—not one particular altar but meaning at the same time the unique altar of the Cross as well as all the altars of our churches—to the eternal sacrifice consummated on the celestial altar which, so says St Thomas, is God himself. (*Summa* III, 83, art. 4.)

And, remarks the same theologian, it cannot mean these eucharistic gifts to be carried to the altar on high in their material form under their appearances of bread or wine, but rather ourselves, the Mystical Body, which is also mysteriously present in these offerings, though in a different way. Thus the eucharistic sacrifice with all that it comprehends, achieves the very end of the redemption and of all salvation: our being transported near to God, our reunion with him, in one body, so that all together and each one of us in particular (*quotquot*) ' May be filled with all heavenly blessing and grace.'

* * *

The Mass is a present, actual everyday sacrifice as concrete and as new each day as the fresh host placed upon the paten, as the wine poured into the chalice and which is not the same wine as yesterday. Each Mass, every morning, is also unique, as fresh and new as the dawn that has just broken, as the flower that has just burst into bloom. But this is a sacramental reality: it utters, it designates, something other than itself. It takes us back to the past, to the mysteries of the historic Christ in which it has its roots, whence it draws all its realness, all its divine vitality. And at the same time it announces, it takes on and impregnates a future in which it will disappear, as the dawn is absorbed by the sun, as the flower sheds its leaves to give fruit. Such is the complex mystery that we have entitled, by a paradox that perhaps by now the reader understands: the memorial of future times.

CHAPTER XIV

MASSES IN SUCCESSION

In order to grasp fully the eschatological import of the Mass, it is not enough to contemplate the mystery of the Mass in itself, as if it were rounded off completely at a single sitting, once and for all. True, the Cross is unique, because Christ died once and for all and his sacrifice was perfect enough to save the whole world; and the Last Supper is unique, because it is the inauguration of a rite. But the rite was instituted in order to be inexhaustibly renewed. In the case of a rite of initiation like baptism, it is only given once to each person. This is seen even more clearly if we consider the baptismal mystery itself; death, resurrection, new birth are all acts which cannot be repeated for the same individual, although the Church goes on repeating them until the end of time for all who are born into the world, to gather them one after the other into the fold. In the Mass, on the other hand, the rite which embodies our Lord's sacrifice and ours, is that of a meal, a taking of nourishment, an action whose very nature demands that it should be repeated indefinitely and frequently. It is the daily bread which the Lord gives us with each new day. For this reason our idea of the Mass and its efficacy will be incomplete if we fail to give some thought to Masses, in the plural, as succeeding one another in time.

* * *

The repetition of the Mass, which at first did not take place daily, is linked up with the weekly recurrence of the ' Lord's Day ', which was instituted by Jesus himself. It was on the first day of the week, the day after the

Sabbath (Matt. 28, 1; Luke 24, 1; John 20, 19), that he appeared to his apostles in his risen body, and shared their meal. After this he disappeared for a whole week. His second appearance took place ' after eight days ', and on this occasion also there was a meal. (John 20, 26.)

The first ' coming of the Lord ', then, had taken place on the first day of the week, soon to be called ' the Lord's Day ' (*Dominica Dies*), within the setting of a brotherly meal, perhaps in that same cenacle where Jesus had instituted the Eucharist and spoken at some length of his departure and return. Preoccupied as they were with the expectation of their Lord's return, the apostles thought that this, like the first appearance, would take place on a Sunday at daybreak, at the same time and on the same day of the week as the resurrection. But Jesus had bidden them ' watch ', so as to be prepared; and so the celebration of the Sunday began on the evening of the previous day (at this period, the day was considered as beginning at sunset.) At first, no doubt, it would have included the lighting of the lamps, the Jewish ritual of the ' lucernarium '. The night was passed in prayer, chanting and listening to the word of God and the homilies of the apostles. This chanting and prayer, these sermons did not serve merely to pass the time and ward off sleep. They opened up the hearts of those present and sustained and developed the ' watchfulness ' of faith and hope. Our Mass of the Catechumens and, no doubt, in part our canonical office, are a heritage from this vigil spent in prayer and the word of God. At dawn the gathering was brought to a close by the ' breaking of bread ', the sacrament of charity. Thus, although the Lord in person had not staged a return, the waiting had not been in vain. The great prayer ' *Maran atha* ' had been answered in its two-fold meaning: ' Come, Lord,' as well as ' The

Lord has come '. They had been waiting, they were still waiting, yet all the time their expectations had already been fulfilled. When morning came, each one returned to his own occupation, strengthened, now, to watch more fervently for the real coming of the Lord, of which the ' Lord's Supper ' was the foreshadowing and the preparation. The name of this meal, too, had a two-fold meaning: if it was no longer the meal to which the Lord would come and take his place in person in the midst of his disciples, as on Easter morning, it was the meal instituted and prepared by him, the meal where he himself gave himself in the form of food, as on the evening of Holy Thursday.

The Roman Liturgy does not appear to have kept this vigil as such, or at least not as a weekly celebration. But the ' weekly Easter ' was soon to give birth to the annual Easter, at which the holy Vigil, ' the mother of all vigils,' would be observed for centuries, then fall into disuse as men lost their sense of the last end; only to be reborn at Easter 1951, through the inspired and providential action of His Holiness Pope Pius XII. Apart from this great Paschal vigil, Rome also practised, several times a year, the ' Pannuchis ', all night prayer, notably for the Ember days, when the entire Community assembled to make an all-night ' station ' for the ordinations. (Just as the Paschal vigil was moved forward to the morning of Holy Saturday, the ' Pannuchis ' of the Ember Days was transferred to the Saturday morning. This explains both the unusual length of the office of this day, and the fact that the proper of the Sunday Mass has had to be made up, as an afterthought, from borrowings from the Masses which precede it.)

The institution of the annual Easter inaugurates the creation of the liturgical year, the mystery of which we shall miss completely if we fail to take into account the mystery of the Eucharistic memory of the passion and resurrection. This renders the entire mystery of Christ present in all its reality, but as a single comprehensive whole. The Church, living in the world of time, a people journeying towards a future life, needs to pick out the separate details of the mystery. This she does by means of the seasons and feasts of the liturgical year. Without the Eucharist these would be a mere series of anniversaries, more or less dramatic, and endowed with great pedagogic value, no doubt, but empty of all reality outside the consciousness of believers. It is the Eucharist which gives to these commemorations their objective, here-and-now reality; the more so since the glorious Christ, who is present in the Eucharist, recapitulates in himself all his earlier mysteries, without their being in any way wiped out by the mysteries which came after them. Whereas a man cannot achieve manhood without ' putting away the things of a child '. (1 Cor. 13, 11.) Christ, on the contrary as he grew to manhood, did not put away the mysteries and states of his childhood, any more than he put away those of his laborious years of manhood, or of his Passion, when he rose again from the dead. (The ' stigmata ' of our Lord's risen body point very distinctly to this aspect of the mystery of Christ.) That is why the Christian meditating on the mysteries of the Rosary can unite himself to the joyful and sorrowful mysteries in spite of the fact that Christ is at present established in his glory and has been so for centuries past. For all that, the ' mysteries ' of the Rosary are not liturgical and never will be. Why? Because each Christian can meditate on them, and live them, as and when he chooses. The liturgical ' mysteries ' on the other hand are lived by the Church at certain definite dates. What is the reason for these dates for each mystery? Simply that the Church, the guardian of the mystery of

her Spouse, celebrates them at those particular dates.
The reality of the liturgical year is based in the first instance
upon the mystery of the incarnate Word. But its final
raison d'être lies in the two-fold and inseparable mystery
of the Eucharist and the Church. Each time the Church
celebrates a feast she utters constantly the same cry:
'Today Jesus is born, is risen, has sent his Spirit upon
the apostles.' This here-and-now reality of each mystery
is derived from the realness of the eucharistic celebration,
and from the power which the Church, assembled for the
occasion, has received, to celebrate, administer and
organise the priestly work of her Spouse.

The feasts, then, are anything but mere commemorations,
a mere matter of conjuring up the past. Still, the question
remains: even if they are, as we have just seen, the celebration of a mystery which is actually present, how are we
to explain their ceaseless repetition? What is the use of
perpetually renewing this cycle which is shut in upon
itself?

In reality the cycle is not shut in at all, and to keep within
the order of geometrical comparisons, it bears less resem-
blance to a circle than to a mounting spiral. Each feast
represents an advance on the corresponding feast of the
previous year, since it brings us nearer to the coming of
Christ, and helps us along on the way to the unique and
perpetual feast which is the life to come. In short, the
liturgical cycle, and each of the feasts and seasons which
make it up, are eschatological.

We often hear it said that Advent is a time for preparing
our souls for Christmas. This is not the case. We know
that Jesus was born at Bethlehem a long time ago, and there
is no point in our trying to mimic the expectation of the
Patriarchs. But his coming at Christmas and his Epiphany
are the figure and the pledge of his final coming: and this

is what Advent prepares us for, as we shall see if we consider the prayers and prophecies of the season.

Again, during Lent, are we waiting for the Resurrection of Christ? Not at all. It took place centuries ago. But in re-living this resurrection by the celebration or renewal of our baptism, we await the coming of Christ, of which the resurrection was the first realisation, and always remains the pledge. Anyone who is reluctant to admit this view of things should re-read attentively the liturgy of Palm Sunday. What we celebrate on this feast is not so much the memory of our Lord's fleeting triumph, as the expectation of his coming and of our entry into Heaven in his train, there to be received by angels, prefigured in the liturgy by the " Hebrew children singing ' Hosannah ' ".

The time after Pentecost is entirely eschatological. It represents the growth of the Church since the disappearance of her Spouse and under the movement of the Holy Ghost. Hence the last Sunday after Pentecost sets before us the account of the end of the word and the coming of Christ as Judge in the clouds of heaven.

From feast to feast, from one Mass to the next, the Church becomes more and more holy, more deeply imbued with the Spirit of Jesus, more completely united in charity; and in this way she draws ever closer to the day of the Lord.

* * *

The postcommunion of the Mass frequently refers to and prays for this growth of the Church. The Church disperses after each Mass, sanctified, beatified and reinvigorated by the Eucharistic meal, and thus better fitted for the celebration of the Eucharist which will bring her members together on the next occasion. From one Mass to the next, she progresses towards the complete union, the perfect charity and the unclouded joy of Heaven.

To conclude this chapter it will suffice to quote some postcommunion prayers, picked out almost at random, which show how the liturgical mystery constitutes a foretaste and a figure of the joys of heaven.

' Let thy faithful, O God, be strengthened by thy gifts: that what they have received they may seek again, and by seeking may receive the same for ever.' (Septuagesima.)

' Fed by the gift of heavenly life we beseech thee, O Lord, that what is to us a mystery in this present life may become our help to life eternal.' (Saturday after Ash Wednesday.)

' Having received, O Lord, these heavenly sacraments, we beseech thy mercy, that what we celebrate here on earth we may attain in everlasting joy.' (Ember Wednesday after Pentecost.)

' Having received these divine sacraments, O Lord, we pray that we may advance towards eternal redemption.' (13th Sunday after Pentecost.)

' May we house in a pure heart, O Lord, what we have received with our lips, so that of the body and blood of our Lord Jesus Christ there may be made for us an everlasting healing.' (Prayer for the ablutions, which was originally a postcommunion.)

Chapter XV

PRAYER FOR PEACE

Those of the faithful who have been brought up on the idea that the Mass is nothing other than the memorial and the renewal of the Passion are in danger of being disappointed when they read the canon of the Mass. What a frigid form of prayer it is, how lacking in pathos and in what people nowadays call ' thrill ' ! How different from the impassioned rhetorical flights of the Good Friday preachers!

The Mass reproduces the Passion, it is true, but under a sacramental mode which is utterly peaceful, by means of bread and wine which are only remotely reminiscent of a body torn by blows and blood spurting under the lashes of a whip. Along with the Passion it re-presents the Resurrection and the Ascension, mysteries of glory and joy. If it contains the sacrifice of Christ, this has become the sacrifice of the Church, so that the prayer which surrounds the sacrifice is not a personal prayer but an ecclesiastical prayer, what we call, precisely, a liturgical prayer. We should add that the Roman liturgy is characterised by sobriety and serenity: there is more dramatic lyricism to be found in the liturgies of the Eastern Church or in the Gallican liturgies of former times.

Being an ecclesiastical prayer, the Mass asks above all for the benefits which are those of the Church, that is to say, of an assembly: unity and peace. (cf.: Secret for the feast of Corpus Christi.) Thus the constantly recurring theme of the Canon of the Mass is the theme of peace.

The first prayer of the Canon refers to the sacrifice 'which in the first place we offer thee for thy holy Catholic Church; deign to *grant her peace*, to protect, unite and govern her throughout the whole world'. Shortly before the consecration in the prayer '*Hanc oblationem*', we find 'We therefore beseech thee, O Lord, favourably to accept this offering . . . . *and to dispose our days in thy peace*'. Again, in praying for the dead, those who '*sleep in the sleep of peace*' we ask for them 'a place of refreshment, light and *peace*.' As the Communion approaches the prayers for peace become more numerous. After the *Pater* the priest develops the last petition: 'Deliver us . . . from all evils . . . and graciously grant *peace in our days*.' Then, almost immediately, after dividing the Host, he sings solemnly 'May the *peace* of the Lord be always with you', and the congregation responds with the same prayer for the priest. The triple '*Agnus Dei*' follows at once, the third invocation ending with '*grant us peace*'. The prayer which follows begins with the words 'Lord Jesus Christ, who dost say to thy apostles "Peace I leave with you, my peace I give unto you", regard not my sins but the faith of thy Church. Deign according to thy will to give her *peace* and unity'. And it is at the end of this prayer that the kiss of *peace* is given, at High Mass, accompanied by the words '*Peace be with you*'.

I have contented myself with picking out the passages where the word 'peace' is actually found. But throughout the Missal the idea of peace is present everywhere. That is the great intention of the Church's prayer, the principal fruit which she hopes to gain from that supreme prayer which is the Eucharistic sacrifice.

When she asks that we may be delivered from all evil, that we may be united to the saints in heaven, that we may

cling to Jesus Christ and never be separated from him, she
is still asking for peace, either under the aspect of security,
or in the positive form of prosperity. The word ' *pax* '
recurs ceaselessly, and we should also notice the number and
variety of terms which express the community or society:
communicantes grex (flock), *numeros*, *consortium* (community
of life), *familia*, *plebs* (people), *ecclesia* (gathering), etc.

* * *

But what peace, precisely, is in question? Are we
praying for peace between nations or peace between
fellow-countrymen? Temporal peace, or spiritual? The
Church does not specify. She says, Peace; that is all. It is
this sobriety of her prayers that gives them their unfailing
appeal to every taste and their limitless adaptability. But
we can say thát there is no kind of peace which her prayer
excludes, and that she regards all peace as supremely good
and desirable.

The Church prays, first of all, for temporal, exterior
peace. Her liturgy was formed at a time when the great
persecutions of the Roman emperors had ceased, but this
brought no assurance of peace. Heresies in those days were
both numerous and violent. (There are heresies still, but
they are less aggressive nowadays, or rather, they are more
widespread, more general.) These heresies were no mere
intellectual tournaments, debates between theologians, or
theses for councils to discuss. Heresy, extremely intolerant,
and often very powerful, was the occasion of murders,
insurrections and exile. To realise this it is enough to read
the life of a St Athanasius or a St Hilary of Poitiers, per-
secuted implacably by Arianism. There was another terrible
danger to peace: the barbarian invasions of the Huns,
Vandals and Lombards. For centuries the Church lived in
terror of invasions. Should we say that she ought not to
have cared about such things, possessing as she did the

promises of eternal life? Or that she desired peace for mere love of an untroubled existence? Not in the least. For her, peace is desirable because without a minimum of security the development of Christian virtues, Christian culture, and Christian worship is impossible. Persecution and war have this in common with poverty; they can, with the grace of God, serve as an opportunity and a springboard for heroic virtues. The Christian way of life, the normal human condition, demands a minimum of well-being for the natural and supernatural development of man.

There is another peace, more supernatural, which the Eucharistic prayer is particularly well-fitted to ask for and obtain, and this is peace between God and humanity. Sin aroused God's anger; it created a state of violence between God and man. Christ came into the world to reconcile us with his Father. This is why St Paul calls Christ not merely the pacific, the peacemaker, but quite simply *our peace*. (Ephes. 2, 14.) Christ is our peace by reason of his sacrifice which, by wiping out the offence, and being acceptable to God, ' pacifies ' God in our regard. How many times, in the prayers of the Mass, we ask God to look upon us with a serene and propitious countenance, to accept our sacrifice. The Eucharist, more than any personal consideration, gives us the certitude of that fundamental peace, of which the angels sang over the cradle of Christ: ' Glory to God in the highest, and on earth peace to men of good will '.

It is still necessary, none the less, that each of us should possess spiritual peace, and know how to still the combat which is waged ceaselessly within himself, and which St Paul describes thus: ' Walk in the spirit: and you shall not fulfil the lusts of the flesh. For the flesh lusteth against the spirit: and the spirit against the flesh. For these are contrary one to another: so that you do not the things that you would . . . . Now the works of the flesh are manifest:

which are fornication, uncleanness, immodesty, luxury, idolatry, witchcrafts, enmities, contentions, emulations, wraths, quarrels, dissensions, sects, envies, murders, drunkenness, revellings, and such like. And the which I foretell you, as I have foretold to you, that they who do such things shall not obtain the Kingdom of God. But the fruit of the spirit is charity, joy, *peace*, patience, benignity, goodness, longanimity, mildness . . . ' (Gal. 5, 16-23.) The whole of the Christian life consists in renouncing the tendencies of fallen nature, in order to strengthen within us the spirit of Jesus. Now in this nothing can help us more powerfully than the Eucharist; firstly because it is the sacrament which gives us the body of Christ for our food, to make us sharers in his spirit. If his spirit really rules us, it will weaken our carnal and violent inclinations and will make us produce fruits of peace and joy. In this way it is the Eucharist which will bring us peace by destroying at the roots the interior divisions which disturb and weary us.

If, thanks to a persevering, frequent and fervent reception of the Eucharist, we have mastered this interior peace, even persecutions coming from without will no longer have any power to touch us. How may saints have undergone the severest trials and borne calumnies and even torture with a smile, because in the love of Christ, quickened by the Eucharist, they had found that peace which the world cannot give, but which it is equally powerless to take away.

If the Christian can draw profit from persecutions in this way, thanks to his unshakable interior peace, that does not mean that he takes no further interest in the cause of peace or that he fails to work for it with all his might. The Eucharist which is the food of his life is the sacrament of fraternal charity. No one can receive the Eucharist with a sincere and generous heart without a firm resolve to root out of his life all jealousy, rancour and egoism. This is the meaning of the petition in the *Pater* which prepares us for Communion: 'Forgive us our trespasses as we forgive them that trespass against us'. This, again, is the meaning of the gesture of the kiss of peace. How can we go up to take our share in the fraternal banquet if we do not love our brethren, if we are not labouring to suppress all the causes of division among men? How can we receive this Sacrament in which we see that Christ has loved us even unto folly, if we do not obey his first and only commandment: 'Love one another as I have loved you'? For Christians who frequent the Eucharist this provides endless matter for examination of conscience.

We see then that the Mass is throughout a prayer for peace, a seed-ground of peace, a living and divine exhortation to build up the edifice of peace within and around us, to the utmost of our power. If Christians truly knew the gift of God, they would possess within themselves that profound peace, accompanied by joy, which is the first-fruit and the first recompense of love; and they would spread peace most effectively all around them: 'Blessed are the peacemakers, for they shall be called the children of God.' (Matt. 5, 9.)

CHAPTER XVI

WORSHIP IN SPIRIT AND IN TRUTH

The first apologists affirmed that Christians had neither temple nor altar. It would be wrong to draw the conclusion that their religion was purely interior, and without any liturgical worship. A spiritualism of that sort would appeal to certain of our contemporaries; being very close to laicism.

The pagans saw in the temple the dwelling-place of God, and their worship centred around sacred places, woods and fountains; the Jewish liturgy could be celebrated only in the temple of Jerusalem, so much so, that during the Babylonian captivity (Dan. 3, 38) and after the sack of the holy city by Titus, the sacrifices ceased altogether, while the Christian sacrifice fulfilled the prophecy of Malachy. (Mal. 1, 11.) ' From the rising of the sun even to the going down . . . in every place . . . there is offered to my name a clean oblation.' The Christian temple is a ' church ': the ' ecclesia ' the assembly of the faithful, who are themselves the ' house of God.' (1 Cor. 3, 16: 2 Cor. 6, 16: Ephes. 2, 19; 1 Pet. 2, 5.) It is enough that ' two or three should be gathered together in his name ' for Christ to be in the midst of them.

The offerings of their sacrifice are no longer goats and bulls; there is no more pouring out of blood, no fat-offerings sizzling in the fire and sending up a smoke for an odour of sweetness; but instead ' spiritual sacrifices ', a giving of thanks (eucharistia) a Church offering herself. The principle of sacrifice is not the gift: it is the soul, the intention behind the gift.

Still, for all that, Christianity is not without its liturgy:
churches which enclose a certain area of material space,
altars of stone, offerings taken from among created things.
Better still, it is Christ himself offering himself, the Incarnate Word, the head of all mankind and the first-born of
every creature, immolating himself in a true sacrifice. The
good which he gives is his flesh, given for the salvation of
the world. It is his blood that is poured out for the remission
of sins. This sacrifice is no mere edifying and instructive
allegory: it is a sacrifice ' in truth '.

The Christian, then, must be present at this sacrifice
where the work of his salvation is both commemorated and
actually wrought. At least every Sunday, every ' Lord's
Day ', he is summoned to the Church where he will be in
communion with the Church, to take part in the visible
sacrifice of his Saviour. His faith is not a mere playing with
concepts, a fabric of ideas, a calling up of ever-fleeting
memories. It becomes incarnate in visible gestures and
resounding words. It rests upon such solid realities as the
altar-stone; it is fed by realities as sustaining as bread and
wine, as living and warm as the flesh and blood of Christ.
It is illumined by the light of candles; it rises to heaven
with the perfume of incense.

But this worship ' in truth ' is also a worship ' in
spirit '. These things are signs. The body of Christ itself,
in its substantial reality is a sign of the body, at once visible
and invisible, which is his Church, made up of a multitude
of members united by charity, in which God will be all in
all at the end of time.

A Christian is, precisely, someone who ' goes to Mass '.
Without that he is no Christian; but that alone is not
enough to constitute him a Christian. The Mass is not a
weekly act of religion which dispenses a man from all the
rest. It is a summit towards which the whole of his daily

life ascends, and from which it re-descends; it is a heart to which and from which everything flows, it is a hearth for which everything is fuel, and by which everything is warmed.

If we have tried, in these pages, to look closely at the rites of the Mass, it is not merely to enable the Catholic to assist at Mass with a good knowledge of what he is doing; it is not merely to give him ' ideas ' about the Mass, but to encourage him to live by the Mass. This sacrifice will be *his* sacrifice only if he brings to its all his efforts of evangelising both himself and others; only if he draws from it the strength he needs for his daily duties; only if he makes it his ' eucharist ' for all the gifts he has received, that is to say, his thanksgiving ' for all things '. (Eph. 5, 20; 1 Thess. 1, 2; 5, 18.)

The Mass should not be an interlude of exterior worship in a spiritual life. The spiritual life is not genuine unless it is nourished by this exterior worship and finds in it its outward and social language. Its effort to practise charity, under pain of falling into mere philanthropy and sentimentality, must come and draw its strength from the ' primary and irreplaceable source of the Christian spirit ' which is, according to Blessed Pius X, the active participation in the liturgy. When St Paul invites his brethren ' by the mercy of God to present their bodies a living sacrifice, holy, pleasing unto God, their reasonable service' (Rom. 12, 1); when St Peter exhorts them to be ' as living stones built up, a spiritual house, a holy priesthood, to offer up spiritual sacrifices, acceptable to God by Jesus Christ ' (1 Pet. 2, 5), they do not imagine that good conduct, resignation in the acceptance of trials, fraternal charity and some efforts to convert the world to Christianity, would in themselves be sufficient to constitute an adequate form of worship. On the other hand they are equally well aware that liturgical worship is not enough to save men's souls and give glory to God unless it finds its continuation in a ' spiritual cult ' by which each one makes Christ's sacrifice his own and makes his own life a prolongation of that sacrifice, according to the demands and graces of his state.

To fail to put the sacrifice of Christ at the heart of the Christian life would be a fault of ' laicism '. But it would be a fault of ' liturgism ' to imagine that all is over and done with once the Mass has been said, and that the community is dismissed, acquitted of all its obligations, by the ' *Ite missa est* '.

We hope that this little book will have made it clear that the incomparable treasure which is the Mass is not meant to be reverently wrapped up in a napkin and buried in a corner. This talent must produce fruit, so that the master, when he returns, may take it back with interest. The true adorers must adore the Father in truth but, because God is a spirit, they must also be adorers in spirit. (John 4, 23, 24.)